THE PRENTICE-HALL SERIES
IN DEVELOPMENTAL PSYCHOLOGY

John C. Wright, editor

Piaget and Knowledge	Hans G. Furth
Piaget for Teachers	Hans G. Furth
Piaget's Theory of Intellectual Development: An Introduction	Herbert Ginsburg and Sylvia Opper
The Cognitive Process: Readings	R. J. C. Harper, C. C. Anderson, C. M. Christensen, and S. Hunka
Readings in Adolescent Development and Behavior	John P. Hill and Jev Shelton
Child Psychology	Wallace A. Kennedy
Psychopathology of Childhood	Jane W. Kessler
Developmental Psychology: A Psychobiological Approach	John Nash

Classroom Behavior

a little book for teachers

DON BUSHELL, JR.

Associate Professor of Human Development and Education
University of Kansas

733883

Prentice-Hall, Inc., Englewood Cliffs, New Jersey

Library of Congress Cataloging in Publication Data

Bushell, Don
  Classroom behavior: a little book for teachers.

  (The Prentice-Hall series in developmental psychology)
  Bibliography: p.
  1. Classroom management.   I. Title.
LB3011.B97   372.1'1'02   73-3421
ISBN 0-13-136275-5
ISBN 0-13-136267-4 (pbk.)

10 9 8 7 6 5 4 3 2 1

Printed in the United States of America

Prentice-Hall International, Inc., *London*
Prentice-Hall of Australia, Pty. Ltd., *Sydney*
Prentice-Hall of Canada, Ltd., *Toronto*
Prentice-Hall of India Private Limited, *New Delhi*
Prentice-Hall of Japan, Inc., *Tokyo*

Contents

Preface

This is a little book about children. It is also about teachers and classrooms; about schools, lessons, and classroom management. Most of all, however, it is about a new art and science called behavior analysis and how it is beginning to change elementary education.

Classroom behavior analysis is not yet ten years old, but in its infancy and early childhood it has accomplished feats to rival the precocious heroics of the legendary Paul Bunyan. Paul was a myth, a fable, a one-time, nonreproducible phenomenon. Behavior analysis is not. What it has accomplished in classrooms throughout the nation during the past few years can be done by you in your own classroom. The pages which follow describe how teachers have accelerated the academic achievements of their children, corrected individual learning problems, and found ways to correct classroom behavior problems without having to rely on outside help from school psychologists, learning disabilities consultants, or guidance counselors.

The discoveries of poverty and racism in America during the 60s were inseparable from the myriad problems of the schools. The

Supreme Court decision of 1954 concerning school desegregation put education in the limelight as never before. Suddenly, that gentle institution which had descended from the quaint little one-room schoolhouse was no longer the home of the town meeting or the symbol of an enlightened settlement. Instead the school became a battleground, the focal point of issues, a prize contested for by this faction and that. Strikes, vandalism, assaults, protests, and the defeat of bond issues tore at the foundations of education, and they also pried the lid off the system far enough for the public to see inside. In many cases the view was not pretty.

Dick and Jane still chased Spot across bolted-down desks with the now useless holes that nestled grandmother's ink well. Too many children jammed the old and ill-equipped classroom that was surveyed by a single teacher. By her own admission, that teacher had often been poorly prepared for the realities of her job. Her professional education at a university or teacher's college had provided theories, apologetics, "methods" curriculum courses and practice with various audio-visual aids, but few were equipped to cope with 30 or more live children on that first frightening day when the door was closed and the theories didn't seem to fit the situation.

School boards toppled, superintendents grew gray and found other professional callings; teachers unionized and, in turn, citizen groups got themselves together to advocate or to protest change. Amidst all this sound and fury it became harder and harder to keep track of the growing number of reformers who offered grand and usually expensive panaceas for the educational system.

It is the thesis of this book that important changes in education can occur only in the classroom. School boards and superintendents will come and go; funding levels will change, and equipment will either be plentiful or scarce; professional organizations will lobby and argue; and "bold experiments" in modular scheduling, ungrading, and open space architecture will know their day in the sun. Withall, nothing will alter the basic fact that real change in education can occur only *inside the classroom.* It is the individual teacher who commands the power to change the system. Administrative authority, laws, and vast sums of money can make things easier or more difficult, but they cannot do the job. The job that must be done can be done only by those who teach children.

Since 1968 a rapidly expanding group of teachers, aides, and parents have been learning, implementing, and adding to the instructional technology based on the principles of modern behavior theory. As a part of Project Follow Through, a federally funded intervention program for poor children, these classroom teams have come to expect new levels of achievement from the children they teach. They have come to expect more because they have experienced the power of their new teaching skills. By their own efforts, these teachers have begun to destroy the predictions that forecast failure for their children.

At the beginning of 1968 there were no books written on the subject of classroom behavior analysis. In those few cases where its primitive techniques were being used, advances occurred because of personal communication and idea exchanges between individuals. Now there are more than a dozen books devoted to discussions of a well-developed, systematic set of procedures which make up behavior analysis. This small book does not attempt to describe the entire field. Instead, it is an introduction to that growing shelf of volumes which are receiving more and more careful attention from administrators and teachers who are responsible for improving the elementary education of children. By the time you have finished this book you will, at the very least, be able to make your own classroom a more productive and enjoyable place to be. You will also be able to decide whether you are interested in learning the more technical and theoretical aspects of behavior analysis. Those who elect to pursue the topic will have little difficulty with more sophisticated materials among those described in the bibliography.

This is not a technical book. Other volumes are assembling the graphs and statistics that document the promise and achievements of behavior analysis programs. The seven chapters that follow are meant to convey the basic notions and practical considerations that animate and give character to the bare framework provided by modern learning theory.

In a very real sense, what follows is a product of work that began at the Student Behavior Laboratory at Webster College in 1965. In January of that year, Patricia Wrobel, Mary Louise Michaelis and Sherrill Bushell opened three experimental classrooms for preschool children. Subsequently, behavior analysis classrooms have multiplied and been improved by the effort, commitment and generosity of a great many people.

Two groups of individuals must be specifically acknowledged. One is composed of my student and faculty colleagues in the Department of Human Development at the University of Kansas. The environment created by their mutual concern has provided bouyant support and sustained encouragement to write this book. The other group is composed of the parents, teachers and administrators throughout the country who have worked with extraordinary skill and dedication to implement Behavior Analysis

Follow Through programs in their several and varied communities. Because of their imagination and hard work, a program that served fewer than 50 children in 1965 is still showing healthy signs of growth as it passes an enrollment mark of 10,000 in 1973. However inadequately, this small volume is meant to acknowledge the contributions these people are making to a promising new design for elementary education.

We are indebted to the following sources for the quotations used in the chapter openings.

Chapter 1 —— *The New York Times Magazine*, March 21, 1971, p. 89.

Chapter 2 —— Barzun, Jacques, *Teacher In America*. Garden City, New York: Doubleday & Company, Inc., 1959, p. 17.

Chapter 3 —— Skinner, B. F., *Science and Human Behavior*. New York: The Macmillan Company, 1953, p. 5

Chapter 4 —— Bruner, Jerome S., *The Process of Education*. Cambridge: Harvard University Press, 1961, p. 88.

Chapter 5 —— Michel de Montaigne, "Of the Education of Children," *Essays I. 25.* in Robert Maynard Hutchins (ed.), *Great Books of the Western World*, *Vol. 25*, p. 73, Chicago: Encyclopaedia Britannica, Inc., 1952.

Chapter 6 —— Russell, Bertrand, *Education and the Good Life*. New York: Liveright Publishing Corp., 1926.

Chapter 7 —— Dewey, John, *Problems of Men*. New York: Philosophical Library, Inc., 1946, p. 192.

1

Teaching

*The fundamental trouble today is
that . . . the schools do not appear
to work.*

Harvey B. Scribner, Chancellor
N.Y. City School System, 1971

Teachers change students' behaviors.

It may be blunt and unglamorous to come right out with it and say that teachers change students' behaviors, but it is sometimes helpful to stress the obvious. Admittedly, these four words do neglect some elements of the teacher's role. In addition to changing students' behaviors, teachers serve as purchasing agents, property clerks, and accident insurance salesmen; they are attendance monitors, playground monitors, hall monitors, and lunchroom monitors; they remain cheerful at faculty meetings and brave when caring for skinned knees and bloody noses; they are audio-visual technicians, janitors, psychologists, revenue collectors for the lunchroom and the *Weekly Reader*, referees for athletic contests, and counselors to parents. Certainly teachers are compassionate exemplars who encourage and inspire, but dwelling on these attributes detracts from the central issue — *pedagogy*.

The teacher as pedagogùe has not received the acclaim and accord enjoyed by the teacher as wise friend or gentle counselor. Perhaps it has something to do with pedagogy's association with the list of methods courses that fail to stand out as intellectual highlights of the teacher's professional training. Although the list of these courses includes the methods of teaching many things, it seldom includes a heading "teaching learning." Since "learning" is the way we describe the *changes* in the way people behave, the intention of the opening four words is to draw attention to the essence of the business.

If you read the opening line, "Teachers change students' *behaviors*," you have encountered a central thesis in all that follows. Like a parent, a teacher is given a limited amount of time to teach a child. A teacher may have the 180 days of a school year to change a nonreader into a beginning reader, or a one-column adder into a two-column adder, but, without a doubt, there is supposed to be some change in the way a student can behave at the end of each year. We have become accustomed to thinking of

3

teaching as a process that develops understanding, improves motivation, promotes creativity, generates insight, and fosters appreciation. All of these are commendable objectives, but each is merely a label which stands for a way in which a child behaves. A student's improved ability to interrelate the complex antecedents of the Civil War in a theme may be labeled "improved understanding," but the quality of "understanding" is always something we must infer from the behaviors we can see. It isn't wrong to talk about a student's understanding. It is just not direct or specific enough.

"*Teachers* change students' behaviors" is a different reading with an additional message. Peers, parents, pets, and playthings may all teach a child, that's true, but whether they do or not does not change a teacher's responsibility. Teachers' professional abilities need to be judged according to how well and how much students learn. The hollow rhetoric about the virtues of teaching appreciation, creativity, insight, and discovery needs to be replaced by clear statements which describe how to teach *children*.

Figure 1-1

Teaching and learning must be linked so that good learning indicates good teaching, and bad learning indicates bad teaching. This is not, however, the rule that is followed in our schools. A variety of very effective barriers have developed which prevent the teacher from assuming full responsibility for the progress of students.

[1] Reprinted with the permission of Fearon Publishers, Belmont, California.

HUNTING SOME SACRED COWS

There are a number of educational practices which, no matter how noble their intentions, have turned out to be "excuses not to teach." If we start with I.Q. scores, we have a nice opening case.

I.Q. Scores

Aside from considerations of what I.Q. scores do or do not measure or predict, they have some clear consequences. When a teacher receives student folders that contain I.Q. scores, she expects the people who scored rather high to learn a lot, those with the average scores are not expected to learn as much, and those with the low scores are not expected to learn very much at all. Consequently, the I.Q. scores tend to reduce the teacher's responsibility to be equally effective with all of the children. The scores can provide an "easy out" which, tragically, is frequently used. If the children with low scores don't achieve well, it is not the teacher's fault, it is the low I.Q. If a teacher expects certain children to bloom during the coming year, they will. Those who have read *Pygmalion in the Classroom* (Rosenthal and Jacobson, 1968) know this is not a new observation. The performance of children will be altered by what the teacher expects of them. Regardless of what an I.Q. score is, it can influence the goals a teacher sets. When lowered expectation reduces the effort a teacher commits to a child, the I.Q. score becomes an excuse not to teach.

Grades

A closely related entry in the "excuse not to teach" category is the custom of grading. It may be the most sanctified practice in education. The usual notion is that students are graded on the basis of what they have learned. That may, however, be the distortion of a direct statement: Grades evaluate what the teacher has taught. A grade distribution is supposed to conform to the distribution of I.Q. scores; both follow a normal curve. When an evaluation of student performance is called for, you are supposed to find that a small portion of the class did very well and they get A's. There is a somewhat larger proportion that did less well and they are given B's. There is the comfortable majority of human beings that did a mediocre job and they get the human grade of C. Those bordering on the outskirts of social acceptability have changed their behavior very little during the period and they get D's. The educational outcasts get F's. Consider the possibility that the teaching procedures used were appropriate for only those students who received A's. For a larger group the procedures were less appropriate and for some students, no effective teaching occurred at all. It is simply not realistic to talk about what students learn as though it is divorced from the way in which they are taught. Nevertheless, the schools' convention of grading has become a wonderful excuse not to teach.

At this point experienced teachers are probably becoming outraged over the apparent assumption that all children should perform equally in similar situations. No such assumption is made. Students, no matter what the grade level, bring different personal histories and different skills into the classroom. No two of them will perform exactly alike. To question the practice of grading is to take seriously the differences among students and to suggest that alternative procedures must be adopted which are both practical and educationally honest.

Ability Grouping (Tracking)

The dangers of grading are worst when the teacher follows a fixed and standard practice for all students (the lecture is the prime example). No matter how clever, the teacher in such a situation winds up presenting information which is too sophisticated for some, too simple for others, and, hopefully, about right for most. One attempt to get around the problem of teaching one group at the cost of depriving another has recently become an excuse not to teach — the track system.

What began as a method for providing more effective education for all students has, instead, in a very casual and natural way, slipped into sets of labels for "ability" groups; labels which influence teacher expectations. If different tracks were designed to be uniquely responsive to the different backgrounds which students bring to the situation, each would use different strategies. A close look at most track systems, however, reveals that the major difference among groups is simply the *rate* at which material is presented. The same books, the same teaching procedures, and the same discussion topics are usually employed for all groups.

The high track group moves through the material rapidly and gets further; the middle track is slower; and the low track group trudges along as best it can. Effective track systems would be expected to display special techniques designed to maximize the progress of the different groups. Most of the existing procedures have, like grading systems, turned out to be institutionalized arrangements for setting different performance standards for various groups. Some are expected to do well — and generally do; others are expected to do less well — and generally do; some are not expected to do very well at all — and they generally comply. For all but the top track, we are faced with another excuse not to teach.

The Bad Environment Dodge

In the teachers' lounge of a low-income neighborhood school one might hear statements like, "You can't really expect too much from Johnny. Terrible home environment. His mother's a hooker and he's never known his father." If anything, a disastrous home environment needs to be offset by a spectacular school environment. Too often, however, teachers who expect less of a child tend to pass over his slow progress rather than stepping up their effort to keep it moving. We have to focus on what the school can do to teach. A teacher can control what happens in a classroom, but has little power to influence a home environment. If a child's lack of progress in the classroom can be blamed on his poor home environment, then the school has developed another excuse not to teach.

Cultural Deprivation

During the past decade, social scientists of honor and repute unwittingly contributed to the growing list a new excuse not to teach. Let us presume that they intended to point up the necessity for special educational strategies to meet the needs of the non-middle-class children in our society who nevertheless attended middle-class oriented schools. They spoke about the "culturally deprived" child, and the label caught on — first in professional journals, and into the popular news media, and finally into the common vocabulary. Without going into the question of what cultural deprivation is or who suffers most from it, it can be seen that within the span of a very few years, what began as an appeal for more sensitive education has become, instead, another excuse not to teach. I have recently heard a teacher explain, "You can't expect as much from these children. They're culturally deprived." There is a scene in *The Miracle Worker* where Miss Sullivan rebukes Helen Keller's father for his indulgence by saying, "I treat her like a seeing child because I ask her to see. I *expect* her to see."

Readiness

Perhaps the most ubiquitous of all excuses not to teach, particularly in primary grades, is the concept of readiness. Here is the capstone of educational double-think. In brief, readiness says, if an attempt is made to teach something to a child and he does not learn it, he is not ready to learn it. Think about it. It has nothing to do with how something is taught. It is the child's fault; he is not ready. A rule can never be faulted which states: when something does not happen, it is not supposed to happen. The system which labels the child not ready can never be judged inadequate. It will always find an excuse not to teach.

A NEW SET OF ASSERTIONS

It is essential that excuses not to teach be rejected in favor of credos that are more optimistic. It is not easy, but it is possible to operate according to different guidelines in the education of young children. The dangers of the self-fulfilling prophecy need not be elaborated for they are well-known to all teachers. Rather than lament the dangers, let us exploit the advantages of new prophecies.

All Children Can Learn

It should not be allowed to pass unnoticed that most children have mastered one of the most complex tasks they will ever face when they learn to communicate in the English language — and they usually have accomplished this before they enter school. If the parents and peers of a particular child started with the assumption that he would never speak, they would probably alter their behavior toward him in the direction of requiring less speech and, thereby, increase the probability that he would remain mute. Happily, everyone assumes that every child will learn how to speak. Operating in blissful ignorance of the principles of behavior, the social environment of virtually every child guarantees that he has the power of conversation all the way to school for his first day of kindergarten. Let our first guide be the assertion that all children can learn.

I.Q. Scores Do Not Indicate How Much A Child Will Learn

I.Q. scores result from the answers which children give to questions. How well they answer questions depends on how much they have been taught, how comfortable they are in a situation where they are required to answer questions, and on how comfortable they are with the person asking the questions. From this it seems to follow that I.Q. scores will be increased by better instruction and by more teaching. To acknowledge that different I.Q. scores reflect different backgrounds and personal histories of experience indicates nothing about the effects of future experiences.

Children Are Different

The most fundamental truth about human behavior plainly requires the abandonment of instructional techniques and conventions of judgment which assume that all children are essentially alike. Uniform presentations by the teacher and grading systems are but two examples of an approach which assumes that every child is pretty much like all other children. Small-group and individualized instruction are requirements for effective primary teaching. The school that admits that these are desirable, but not possible, is not keeping up with the times. Programmed instruction, peer-tutors, paraprofessional aides, self-instructional devices, and the independent work skills of the children can all be marshalled to enable varying degrees of individualized instruction. The day of the one-room schoolhouse is not gone. Every successful teacher has learned to cope with the reality that there is a wider range of skill and experience within any second-grade class than between the second grade and the first or third grade.

Labeling Children Is Usually Dangerous

The tyranny of the self-fulfilling prophecy is too often demonstrated in "modern" schools which have discovered countless psychological, sociological, economic, neurological, physiological, audiological, dietary, developmental, motivational, cultural, and genealogical reasons why children do not learn. Virtually without exception, the labels which are attached to children are used to describe a set of conditions; they *do not explain* what or how a child will learn. The difference between description and explanation deserves attention.

It is easy to fall into the trap of treating a descriptive term as though it is a causal statement. The following citation provides an example:

> "The teacher who observes eight-year-old Jimmy constantly fighting with other children is concerned with understanding or explaining his behavior in order that she might attempt to change it. For a school psychologist to say that Jimmy is constantly fighting because he is a hostile-aggressive child may sound very impressive, but it really adds no new knowledge, for if we ask how one knows that this is a hostile-aggressive child, the reply is that the child is always fighting. The term "hostile-aggressive," then, is only another name for "one who is always fighting." It does not explain the behavior or indeed add any new information, if the only ways of observing "hostility" are in the behavior itself. In the end, the statement that "Jimmy fights because he is hostile-aggressive" proves to be a tautology: "Jimmy fights because he fights."[2]

Try it yourself. The procedure is quite simple. First, describe a problem behavior.

"Little Sally doesn't stay interested in anything for more than a few moments."

"Why not?"

"Because she has a very short attention span."

"What makes you say she has a short attention span?"

"Because . . . . . (complete the sentence in 15 words or less).

Here are some others to practice with:

[2] Staats, A. W. and Staats, C. K., *Complex Human Behavior*, New York: Holt, Rinehart and Winston, Inc., 1964, p. 16.

Bob isn't motivated.

Carol hasn't broken the reading code.

Ted is hyperactive.

Alice is dislexic.

Labels which describe characteristic behavior patterns do not explain the behaviors and they are often irrelevant to changing them.

Children Can Learn In Spite Of Catastrophic
Home Environments

It is a clear and tragic fact that millions of children come to school from home situations that would be best described by Charles Dickens. It is also a fact that this condition need not destroy a child's ability to learn effectively in the classroom. What children do or do not learn in the classroom depends on what and how well they are taught in the classroom. Even the absence of impressive learning in one classroom does not necessarily foretell the absence of progress in another.

A few years ago, three applied researchers established an after-school remedial program for inner-city sixth-grade children who had a lot going against them (Wolf, Giles, and Hall, 1968). For the most part the children were from welfare families of more than five children with no father at home. The sixteen children had a median I.Q. score of 88, a grade average of D, and they were all reading at least two years below the norm for their grade level on the *Stanford Achievement Test.* For the previous two years, these children had gained an average of 0.6 years per year on this test.

After a year of effective instruction in this unique classroom, these children gained 1.5 years on the *Stanford Achievement Test* (twice as much as the control group), increased their grade average in regular school a full letter grade (no gain by the controls), and enjoyed the program so much they voted to have class on every holiday when they were allowed the choice. (On Thanksgiving and Christmas they were not allowed to choose because the *instructors* didn't want to work.)

This special program, directed by Montrose Wolf, David Giles, and Vance Hall is a powerful demonstration that in spite of unfavorable home situations, low I.Q. scores, and a history of failure in public school, these children had a *very* successful year.

Readiness Is Taught

This final assertion is not as daring as it appears. It merely acknowledges that *readiness* is usually a shorthand way of describing a collection of skills which are a prerequisite to a more complex skill. The space program used Mercury and Gemini series to get *ready* for the Apollo trips to the moon. The early efforts helped develop the skills needed for successful moon exploration. When the techniques of propulsion, guidance, telemetry, and life support were mastered, we were ready to go to the moon. Children are ready for handwriting when they are able to follow simple instructions, sit in a chair for a few minutes, hold a pencil in the approved way, and tell when the mark they make is similar to the example provided. Each of these is a teachable behavior. When all of them have been taught, the child is ready for handwriting.

The human organism is virtually complete at birth. There is a lot of folklore around suggesting that capacities develop with age, but it is just that — folklore. Anyone who has watched a preschool age child deftly remove the legs from an ant would be hard pressed to imagine that the same child lacks the "fine motor control" required to hold a pencil. Regardless of age, muscles need training and practice to achieve tone and coordination. The real issue is whether that training and practice should occur by accident in the normal course of childhood activity or whether it should be provided purposefully and systematically in the classroom. Some teachers wait until children are ready. Others *get them ready!*

WHY CHANGE?

The time has come to recognize a truth about our educational system. It is failing. By any set of democratic standards, the conclusion must be the same. The sentence of failure is a pill which goes down hard and many examples of grand prose have contributed to a glowing eulogy eloquently leading us to the conclusion that, even if unrealized, the ambitions of our educational system are far too noble to demean with criticism. As survivors of this system, we affectionately defend the ark, our dearly remembered school, and quietly persist in suggesting that its critics are arrogant, self-seeking and not properly respectful of their own backgrounds. Indeed, how could any system be criticized which has so successfully produced such articulate critics?

Society's requirement that schools teach our children is not being met. The facts are now written too boldly to be hidden, to be disguised by sentiment, or to be obscured by the twin sins of ignorance and complacency! There is no need to present columns of figures and facts to come to the conclusion that something is not right. We must live with the facts. To further ignore them will surely amplify the catastrophe. We are literally surrounded by fifth-grade students who are reading at the preprimer level. Children who lack reading skill when they are in the fifth grade have virtually no chance for survival in the schools. We record with fidelity and a clear round hand the numbers describing the growing rates of dropouts, school vandalism, truancy, and delinquency. Great quantities of energy and ingenuity are focused on building a gigantic testimony to the failures of the schools — I refer to the proliferating catalog of programs in Special Education, Compensatory Education, and Remedial Education. Regardless of their titles, virtually all of these desperate attempts to compensate for the schools' teaching failures rely on the same teaching methods which were unsuccessful in the first place. In the midst of a technological society that demands great skill, teaching methods are perpetuated which do not predictably teach. In launching a government "attack on illiteracy," former U.S. Commissioner of Education, James E. Allen, Jr., indicated that one-fourth of the nation's students have significant reading deficiencies and there are more than three million adult illiterates in America. If, as H. G. Wells observed, history is a race between education and destruction, it would appear that we had better hurry up a little faster.

To criticize weakness without simultaneously providing practical recommendations for improvement is bad form. To criticize public schools is about as sportsman-like as shooting fish in a barrel with a cannon load of grapeshot. I have no interest in becoming another educational critic beyond the point of acknowledging those grotesque data which testify that our schools are not succeeding at their task. At the opening of a new decade school boards are contracting with private industry to operate their classrooms. When the sword of leadership is yielded in such a flamboyant gesture of defeat, no further criticism is possible.

WIDE RANGE ACHIEVEMENT TEST

SPRING POSTTEST SCORES 1969, 1970, 1971

BEHAVIOR ANALYSIS

NON B.A. COMPARISON GROUP

READING

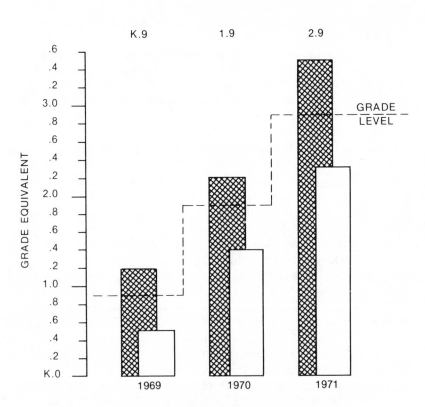

Figure 1-2

14

CHANGE TO WHAT?

Figure 1-2 explains the reason for all that follows. There is a better way to teach. The two groups of children described by the graph are from the same neighborhood and ordinarily would be expected to make similar progress in school. However, one group of 32 children is advancing at the rate of about five or six months' gain in achievement per school year, while the other group of 39 children is moving out at more than twice that rate. The teaching system enjoyed by the rapidly moving group is the subject of the following chapters. This is not just a hypothetical system; real children are responsible for the graph shown in figure 1-1. These children are profiting from a practical set of procedures which are already being employed by hundreds of teachers in classrooms throughout the nation.

The system does exist and it is altering the educational careers of thousands of young children. The teachers using the approach have not had to change their personalities, or be born again. They have turned their classrooms right side up again so that what children learn is viewed as the direct measure of a teacher's effectiveness.

Supported by a new understanding of human learning, these teachers are demonstrating that the job of the teacher, after all, is to change students' behavior.

REFERENCES

Rosenthal, Robert and Lenore Jacobson, *Pygmalion in the Classroom*, New York: Holt, Rinehart and Winston, Inc., 1968.

Staats, Arthur W., and Carolyn K. Staats, *Complex Human Behavior*, New York: Holt, Rinehart and Winston, Inc., 1964.

Wolf, Montrose M., David K. Giles, and R. Vance Hall, "Experiments with token reinforcement in a remedial classroom." *Behavioral Research and Therapy*, 1968, *6*, 51-64.

2

Some Principles

of Learning/Teaching

All the knowledge, skill, art, and science that we use and revere, up to Einstein's formulas about the stars, is a mere repetition and extension of the initial feat of learning to walk.

Jacques Barzun, 1945

Because the process of teaching is meant to change students' behaviors, it is useful to understand something of the lawful and regular ways new behaviors are learned. Until very recently, systematic learning theories were only interesting and useful to educational researchers. In the past few years, however, more and more school districts have begun to evaluate how the *products* of modern behavior theory can respond to what Charles E. Silberman has labeled the *Crisis In The Classroom* (1970). The product of interest to teachers is a set of procedures known as *behavior analysis teaching.*

Behavior analysis is an extension of the experimental analysis of behavior, the laboratory science of learning associated with the name of B. F. Skinner (1938, 1953, 1968). Since the late 1930s, the experimental analysis of behavior has been busily compiling a list of fundamental principles which account for much of human behavior and learning. Fortunately, a basic orientation to the strategies of behavior analysis does not require an exhaustive examination of the entire range of behavioral principles. The essential wisdom of the science can be told, for the most part, through a description of the teaching procedures it has generated.

THREE TYPES OF CONSEQUENCES

The experimental analysis of behavior has focused particular attention on the way that behavior is affected by its immediate *consequences.* The word "consequence" does not refer to possible long range effects of behavior, and it does not have any implication of sanction (as with "Truth or Consequences"). Technically, a consequence is a change in the environment which *immediately* follows a person's act, or behavior. Different changes (different consequences) determine how the behavior which preceded them is going to be altered. In behavior analysis, a consequence is classified according to the effect it has on a behavior.

Behavioral consequences occur in a variety of combinations and according to different schedules, but, regardless of the mixture or arrangement, they can be placed into one of three basic categories.

Reinforcers — Consequences That Strengthen Behavior

First is the consequence which has the effect of *increasing* the strength or frequency of the behavior which it follows. Imagine the boy who puts his hand in a cookie jar and finds a cookie. Finding a cookie is the kind of consequence that is very likely to strengthen the behavior (increase the frequency) of reaching into the cookie jar. Similarly, the behavior of a child saying, "Teacher, teacher, look at this," is likely to be increased by the consequence of the teacher turning to say, "That's very nice, Alan." *Any* consequence which has the effect of strengthening a behavior is called a *reinforcer*. In fact, an event can only be called a reinforcer if it actually increases the strength or frequency of the behavior it follows. The teacher's compliment, "Billy, that was very good. Thank you," immediately following Billy's offer to share his truck with another child can only be called reinforcing if Billy's cooperative play increases as compliments continue.

Punishers — Consequences That Weaken Behavior

If, when reaching for a cookie, the boy encountered a mouse trap snapping shut on his fingers, it is not likely that this consequence would be a reinforcer. Quite the opposite, if this happens often he is likely to pull his hand back rather quickly whenever he even sees a cookie jar. The strength of the "reaching into the jar" behavior is decreased. Consequences of the sort provided by mouse traps are likely to have that effect. Any consequence which has the effect of *decreasing* the strength (decreasing the frequency) of a behavior is technically called a *punisher*. Like reinforcers, punishers can only be defined by the effect they have on a behavior.

Is scolding a punisher? For most children it is, but you really can't say for sure unless you observe a decrease in the strength of the behavior that gets scolded.

Noise — Consequences That Don't Change Behavior

The third type of consequence may be the most common in some classrooms. It has *no* effect on the behavior it follows. Gold stars on charts and papers have often been used by teachers to acknowledge good work. Is a gold star a reinforcer? Most teachers have decided that gold stars seem to help with some children, but mean nothing to others. For some children the stars are reinforcers, for many others they are irrelevant. They neither strengthen nor weaken the behavior for which they are given. Because they have *no* effect, they are just so much noise in the system.

Monday, 9:15 a.m.:	"Charlie, the next time you do that you're going to the principal's office."
Tuesday, 10:00 a.m.:	"Charlie, if you do that again, you're going straight to Mr. Frederick's office."
Friday, 9:45 a.m.:	"Stop that, Charlie."
Friday, 2:10 p.m.:	(Friday is not Charlie's day.) "Charlie, the next time you do that you're going to march right down to the office."

About the only thing to be said about the consequences this teacher is applying to Charlie's behavior is that they are noisy. Her threats and commands are certainly not punishers because the frequency of his inappropriate behavior is not decreasing. It is almost too easy to think of examples of neutral consequences. Comments that are repeated often without any apparent effect on children's behavior usually include: "Hurry up." "Quiet in the halls." "Raise your hand." "Don't talk out." "Hurry up." "Don't forget to do your homework." "Hurry up." "Face front and don't bother your neighbor." "Quiet in the halls." Indeed, the fact that these comments are heard so often suggests that they may be strengthening (reinforcing) the behavior they are intended to weaken.

Effect vs. Intent

A consequence can only be defined as reinforcing or punishing if it strengthens or weakens a behavior. This requirement gives a very precise meaning to the word "reinforce." The word reward does not fit the definition, for it refers to the intention of the teacher rather than to an effect on the student's behavior. A teacher may intend to reward a child with a gold star, but unless it strengthens the behavior that earns it, the gold star is not a reinforcer. A doting grandmother comes to the house and rewards her grandson with a big hug and a kiss. If grandson takes a dim view of such mush it may only reinforce getting out of the house when grandmother arrives.

Similarly the technical use of punisher and the common use of the same word are quite different. A teacher may intend to punish a student by saying, "Sit down and stop talking out of turn," but unless that admonishment weakens those inappropriate behaviors, it cannot be declared a punisher. Indeed, one study (Madsen, et al., 1968) showed that the more frequently first grade teachers asked their children to sit down, the more frequently they stood up! It was only when the children were praised for sitting and working that the frequency of standing up was reduced. No matter what the intention of the teacher in this case, "sit down" commands had the *effect* of reinforcing standing up!

Contingencies

So far, two basic components of behavior analysis, a *behavior* and its *consequence*, have been the center of attention. The reasoning is very direct:

    a. Teachers change students' behaviors.

    b. Behaviors are changed by their consequences.

    c. Therefore, teachers change students' behaviors by managing the consequence of classroom behavior.

The relationship between a behavior and its immediate consequence is so important there is a special jargon word for it, *contingency*. Familiar statements of contingency are "if . . . then . . ." If this behavior occurs, then this consequence will follow; if that behavior, then another consequence. You have contingency plans. If this happens you'll do one thing; if that happens you'll do something else. I find a cookie contingent on (as an immediate consequence of) reaching into the jar.

The experimental analysis of behavior has discovered that certain contingencies influence behavior in standard and predictable ways. Being able to manage contingencies allows certain behaviors to be strengthened and others to be weakened. The careful and precise arrangement of contingencies enables a teacher to be more effective in changing the behavior of students — to be a more effective teacher.

TWO STAGES OF LEARNING

Defining teaching as the task of changing behavior implies that changes in behavior constitute learning. That's right, they do. The implication can be confirmed by examining the way that different patterns of consequences generate different changes in behavior, different types of learning.

Generalization: Getting Things Started

One type of learning is so patterned and so predictable that it has a special name, *generalization*. Technically, when a behavior that has been learned (reinforced) in one situation happens in other similar situations, generalization has occurred. The fact that behaviors do generalize means that when a behavior is learned it is available in a variety of similar settings and it is not necessary to learn a new set of behaviors for each new situation.

A familiar example of generalization is provided by the very young child who is just learning to say "Daddy" when his father comes into the room. During the early stages of this learning, the child is very likely to say "Daddy" to the grocer, the mailman, the druggist, and any other male who happens to be around. This may be embarrassing for the mother and the strange men, but it is a nice sign that the behavior of saying "Daddy" in the presence of males has been learned. At this point the behavior is generalized to all men, so the learning is not completely appropriate, but the process has begun.

Another example of generalization can be drawn from the experience of all those who learned to drive a car that had a clutch and a gear shift. If that kind of car was the only type driven for some time, the clutch behavior undoubtedly generalized to the first encounter with an automatic shift car. There are many similarities between both types of cars, so the act of depressing the clutch generalizes from the early experience and the result is frantic pounding with the left foot against the floorboard followed by, "excuse me." The previous reinforcement provided by timely clutching has taught a behavior which has generalized even though it is no longer appropriate.

Young children learn how to handle a crayon well enough to make a mark and, without special precautions, that behavior sometimes generalizes all over the walls, floor, and their own shoes. Reinforce a child for saying "A" when you hold up that letter, and that behavior will first generalize so the child will say "A" to every letter you hold up. Reinforce the behavior of saying "red" in response to the question, "What color is this?" and, for a while, that question will always be answered "red" regardless of the actual color presented.

In all of these cases, reinforcement has developed a generalized behavior which is not under very precise control. Therefore we must meet the next requirement. The stomping foot needs to come under the precise control of the clutch pedal; "Daddy" needs to come under the control of the unique characteristics of one man; writing with crayons needs to be specifically associated with coloring books and paper to the exclusion of walls and shoes.

Discrimination: Building A Specific Prompt

When the behavior of pushing the left foot down occurs when there is a clutch pedal present, and does not occur when a clutch pedal is absent, *discrimination* has occurred. The difference is that now the behavior of pushing the foot down is specifically determined by (under the control of) the clutch pedal rather than by the general characteristics of the car. The presence of the clutch pedal *prompts* a particular behavior. In the presence of a clutch, pushing your left foot down correctly is reinforced by the immediate consequence of smooth acceleration. In the absence of the clutch, pushing your foot down has no reinforcing consequences. This is the process which is always responsible for bringing a generalized response under the specific control of a particular prompt. *A prompt is an event or object which is always present when a behavior is reinforced, and when it is absent, the behavior is not reinforced.*

Most doors have knobs on them, and, through long training and experience, we have learned that the response of reaching for the knob and turning it will result in the reinforcing consequence of access to the next room. A push plate on the door, however, is a prompt for a very different response. Reaching for and trying to turn a push plate is just not going to be reinforced; pushing on the plate will be. Even on otherwise identical doors, the differences provided by hardware come to control different behaviors. We learn to behave differently because we have been reinforced for different behaviors toward knobs and push plates. In order to realize how very strongly such bits of brass prompt certain behaviors you only need to watch people encounter those occasional doors which have both a knob and a push plate. If only the knob works on such a door, you will witness a number of people in a hurry crumpling into an unyielding barrier.

Classrooms prompt certain kinds of behaviors. All rooms share many properties, but there are also characteristics which are unique to classrooms: blackboards, certain kinds of furnishings, and even familiar odors. In the past, when these features were present, certain behaviors were reinforced and others were either ignored or forbidden. Similarly, people do not behave the same way at a football game as they do in church — most churches and most football games. Each setting prompts different behaviors. Consequently, it is not surprising that children frequently behave very differently at school than they do at home. Neither is it surprising that you don't converse the same way over the telephone as you do over a cup of coffee.

The symbol 4 is a prompt for saying "four." That is the only response it is supposed to control. You are not reinforced for saying "seventy-eight" in the presence of a 4, nor for saying "four" when presented with the symbol 78. If all has gone well, each symbol prompts one particular behavior and no others. How quickly this comes about depends on how often reinforcement has been provided for the behavior of saying "four" in the presence of a 4 and "seventy-eight" in the presence of 78.

A teacher prompts in order to set the occasion for a particular behavior. A question is a prompt for an answer; printing on a page prompts reading, blanks on a quiz prompt written answers, crayons and paper prompt coloring, "Good morning," from the teacher prompts "Good morning," in reply, and the signal to end one activity prompts putting things away in preparation for the next activity. If appropriate behaviors are reinforced when these prompts occur, the prompts will become more and more effective in producing appropriate behavior. This is what we mean by behavioral control. The establishment of that control and its transfer to increasingly complex and subtle prompts is what classroom learning is all about.

THE LEARNING EPISODE:
BASIC UNIT OF INSTRUCTION

Behavior analysis is the evaluation and modification of three types of events and their relationships:

PROMPT - BEHAVIOR - CONSEQUENCE

As the minimum set of elements present in any learning situation, these three events combine to constitute a learning episode. Every instructional process can be analyzed in terms of the arrangement of these three-part learning episodes, and the remainder of the book will focus on just that.

The Development Of A Prompt

Consider the opening days of a first grade class (early levels are best for illustration because there is a limited history of student experience to confound things). The teacher wants to work with a small reading group of seven children in a certain part of the room (the reading corner). She has not had a reading lesson with this group before.

> The time is 9:10. The previous 25 minutes have been devoted to opening exercises, lunch count, and "what song shall we sing today?" It's early October and everyone decides to sing *Jingle Bells.*
>
> To start this first lesson, the teacher calls each of the seven children by name and asks them to join her in the reading corner. Each child leaves his "seat work," joins the teacher, and, for the next 20 minutes, a good time is had by all. Within a very few days, a visitor to that same classroom at 9:10 hears the closing notes of a song (*Jingle Bells* again), and then sees a group of seven children join the teacher as she seats herself beside a large chart and opens a book on her lap. No spoken instructions, no personal invitations to the children are observed, but the transition from one activity to the next is smooth, and "Group 1" has started its daily reading lesson.

The ten times that the reading group has assembled have constituted ten learning episodes. The reinforcing consequence of joining the group for the first time not only strengthened the behavior of going the second time, it also began to make prompts out of the conjunction of two events. The end of the song, combined with the teacher's move to a certain position in the room with a certain book, set the occasion for seven children to join her. That combination of events was not a prompt on the first or second day, but very soon it was. How soon, depends on how much reinforcement the teacher provided for quickly joining the group. Further, the same events soon prompt the remaining children in the class to engage in some other activity. The reinforcing consequences of joining the reading group in the presence of certain events have turned these events into effective prompts for going to reading for the children in that group.

> *Rule:* The more often a behavior is reinforced in the presence of a specific event, the more quickly that event will become a prompt for that behavior.

Differential Reinforcement

The seven readers in Group 1 above have been effectively reinforced by the teacher's approval and attention for quickly joining the group. Suppose, however, one child was unusually slow in getting himself together and joining the group for its eighth lesson. In too many classrooms the subsequent course of events is painfully predictable. The teacher would turn to Sam, the dawdler, with a firm, "Hurry up, Sam, we are all waiting to begin." It is a common error, and an easy one to make, but a serious error nevertheless. Sam's dawdling has drawn the immediate consequence of teacher attention. Teacher attention is usually a reinforcer. Sam's dawdling is being reinforced! On successive days, Sam can be expected to be slower and slower to arrive; and the teacher can be expected to increase her urging that Sam "move it along." Sam's next report card will probably show a low mark on "cooperativeness."

When several different behaviors are reinforced equally, each is going to be strengthened. The trick is to establish strong *differential reinforcement* for one specific behavior by making sure that all other behaviors have less reinforcing consequences. One behavior may result in more reinforcement or faster, more immediate reinforcement than others, but a clear differential is essential.

> *Rule:* The stronger the differential reinforcement, the more quickly behavior will change (the more quickly competing behaviors will be reduced).

Applying the rule to Sam's behavior would lead the teacher to resist all temptation to attend to him. Instead, she would completely ignore his tardy arrival and immediately begin the lesson by giving complete attention and enthusiastic praise to the six children present. When Sam finally does arrive, his participation also earns praise and approving attention. The differential is established. Sam's behavior outside of the group does not result in positive reinforcement; his behavior in the group does. He is not likely to be anywhere else if he has the opportunity to be in the group.

Unfortunately, suggesting that a teacher ignore a noncompliant child is almost like suggesting to water that it run uphill. If there is any tactical error which is committed more than any other in a classroom it is the amount of attention teachers give to inappropriate behavior. As with the children mentioned earlier who stood up more often when the teacher told them to "sit down," inappropriate attention eliminates the differential so vital to effective reinforcement. Worse, it can turn the whole procedure around.

When a standing child momentarily sits following the teacher's command, his subsequent standing is likely to be reinforced by her attention, and her subsequent commanding is likely to be reinforced by his immediate response of sitting. Insidious, isn't it? The child is teaching the teacher to command and the teacher is teaching the child to stand. By attending to Sam's dawdling, the teacher could quickly compound the problem. Instead, by withholding all reinforcing attention from Sam's dawdling, and providing it *only* for his participation, the teacher saves her energy for the business of teaching and avoids later problems.

The different ways that prompts and consequences can be arranged and combined make up a complete index of instructional tactics and strategies. The most fundamental arrangement of learning episodes, as well as the most complex, can always be analyzed in terms of how the prompt, behavior, and consequence are arranged and combined.

A Basic Combination Of Learning Episodes: Shaping

Learning episodes can be arranged with almost endless variation, but some patterns are so common that they have special labels. One such pattern is labeled *shaping*.

Shaping is technically defined as "the differential reinforcement of successive approximations of a final performance." The phrase has just the right kind of ring for a scientific definition, but an illustration can help describe the process. As you read the following example, remember that shaping is possible because of an important behavioral, or even biological, fact: *behavior normally occurs with slight variations.* Almost anything a person does, no matter how subtle, is somewhat different on each occurrence. The act might be faster, slower, larger, smaller, smoother, or jerkier. Whatever dimension of the action we decide to observe, variations along that dimension can be measured. Like snowflakes, no two instances of a behavior are exactly alike.

A first grade teacher is concerned because whatever activity Charlie engages in, he seems to tire of it in just a few moments (the famous "attention span" problem). In her judgment, Charlie needs to learn to stay with a chosen task in the reading corner for at least fifteen continuous minutes before she can expect him to profit from a beginning reading lesson. She decides to "teach" him to have a longer attention span.

Step 1: Define The Problem By Counting Something. The teacher was pretty sure that Charlie's attention span is low, but she realized she may just have noticed him when he was moving and not when he was quietly engaged in some activity. To make sure of her initial judgement, she decided to keep a record of Charlie's behavior through two hours of one day. The record was a simple tally sheet. Each time Charlie began an activity (opening a book in the reading corner, getting a book off the shelf, etc.) she glanced at her watch. When he stopped that activity and moved to another, she noted the elapsed time and entered a tally mark beside the appropriate number of minutes. At the end of the day, her record looked like Figure 2-1.

Her suspicions are confirmed. Although Charlie stayed with one activity for ten continuous minutes, most of his on-task intervals were about five minutes and twice he changed activities in less than one minute.

Step 2: Create A Favorable Situation. Because it was easy to observe

Name: _CHARLIE QUICK_

Date: _OCT. 12_

Behavior: _"ON TASK" IN READING CORNER_

1 min.	//
2 min.	
3 min.	//
4 min.	///
5 min.	//// //
6 min.	//// /
7 min.	//
8 min.	/
9 min.	
10 min.	/
11 min.	
12 min.	
13 min.	
14 min.	
15 min.	
16 min.	

Figure 2-1

and record, the teacher decided to strengthen Charlie's behavior of looking at books in the reading corner. She had seen him spend five or six minutes in this way on several occasions so she knew she would not have to wait long for the behavior to occur.

Step 3: Select An Effective Reinforcer. During the first month of school the teacher had discovered that Charlie, like most of her children, was very responsive to her attention and approval (adult social attention is a powerful reinforcer for most young children). She decided to use the carefully timed delivery of her attention to reinforce Charlie's activity in the reading corner.

Step 4: Strengthen The Behavior (Shape). The first opportunity to respond to Charlie came almost immediately. After he had been looking through some books for five minutes, she joined him with a compliment about how nicely he was "reading" and she stayed with him long enough to read him the captions under a couple of pictures.

During a later period, Charlie didn't enter the reading corner, so she carefully avoided saying anything at all to him. Later, however, Charlie did open a book again. She waited for six minutes this time, and then she invited two of the other children to join them and she read all three a story from a book which Charlie selected.

On successive occasions, the teacher gradually raised the requirement for the length of time Charlie needed to stay "on-task" before she praised and attended to him. From seven minutes, to eight, to ten, then twelve, her reinforcing comments were successively applied to closer and closer approximations of her fifteen-minute goal. Within a few days, Charlie was reliably spending fifteen-minute intervals in the reading corner, and occasionally longer. Having taught (shaped) an increased attention span, the teacher decided to include Charlie in the daily reading lesson.

Each time an improvement in a child's behavior results in *immediate* reinforcement, there arises a new distribution of behaviors, and some of them are closer to the desired goal. By reinforcing each new improvement as it occurs, still further improvements are made more probable, and the shaping process can advance yet another step. Now, let's look at the definition again: *Shaping is the differential reinforcement of successive approximations of the final performance.*

The elements of the shaping process are so basic, so fundamental to any instructional routine, that the word "shaping" is an excellent synonym for TEACHING. The shaping process is the key element in a series of well defined steps which can be clearly stated. All of the steps were illustrated in the preceding account of Charlie's rise to success, but they are not limited to such situations. Indeed, arranging the five steps in order provides a complete outline of the Behavior Analysis Model for Teaching.[1]

The Behavior Analysis Model for Teaching

1. SPECIFY THE FINAL PERFORMANCE, AND DEVELOP A WAY TO MEASURE IT.

2. DETERMINE THE STUDENT'S CURRENT PERFORMANCE LEVEL.

3. CONSTRUCT A FAVORABLE LEARNING SITUATION.
   a. Provide prompts for appropriate behavior.
   b. Eliminate prompts for inappropriate behavior.

4. ESTABLISH MOTIVATION.
   a. Identify the students' reinforcers.
   b. Construct a system for the contingent delivery of reinforcers.

5. SHAPE.
   a. Reinforce successive approximations of the final performance.
   b. Gradually raise the criterion for reinforcement.

REFERENCES

Madsen, C.H., Jr., W. C. Becker, D. R. Thomas, L. Koser, and E. Plager, "An analysis of the reinforcing function of sit down commands," in R. K. Parker (ed.), *Readings in Educational Psychology.* Boston: Allyn & Bacon, 1968.

Silberman, Charles E., *Crisis In The Classroom: The Remaking of American Education.* New York: Random House, 1970.

Skinner, B. F., *The Behavior Of Organisms.* New York: Appleton-Century-Crofts, 1938.

————, *Science and Human Behavior.* New York: Macmillan, 1953.

————, *The Technology of Teaching.* New York: Appleton-Century-Crofts, 1968.

---

[1]Adapted with the permission of the author and publisher from Ellen P. Reese, "The analysis of human operant behavior," in J. Vernon (ed.), *Introduction to Psychology: A Self-Selection Textbook,* Dubuque, Iowa: Wm. C. Brown Company, 1966, p. 49.

3

Objective

Progress Records

*If we can observe human behavior
carefully from an objective point
of view and come to understand it
for what it is, we may be able
to adopt a more sensible
course of action.*

B. F. Skinner, 1953

The first step in behavior analysis teaching is to describe what behavior the student should be able to perform after completing an instructional sequence. The idea is not a new one. Countless inservice workshops have wrestled with defining instructional objectives ever since Robert Mager (1962) published his clever programmed text on the subject several years ago. With elegant style, Mager made several points which are now widely accepted by educators. First, he established that unless you know where you are going, you are likely to end somewhere else. In other words, unless you know exactly what the final performance should look like, there is no way to recognize and reinforce an approximation — no way to shape.

State The Objective Behaviorally

Mager also insisted on stating instructional objectives in behavioral terms. A final performance must be something which a student DOES, not what he "feels," "appreciates," "understands," or is "aware of." Unless knowledge and appreciation are translated into observable behaviors there is no way to decide whether or not a student has reached the instructional goal. Mager put it quite bluntly, ". . . if you are teaching skills which cannot be evaluated, you are in the awkward position of being unable to demonstrate that you are teaching anything at all." (1962, p. 47) Another way of making the same point is to note that *every instructional objective must include a measurement procedure.*

A measurement might come from a paper-pencil performance, a recitation, or a problem solution. When Charlie's teacher decided to increase his attention span the instructional goal and its measurement were established together — fifteen minutes of continuous attention. This statement of the goal guided her delivery of attention and praise and also indicated how to measure Charlie's improving behavior. The same procedure was used to measure Charlie's final performance, his initial performance, and his daily progress.

Determine The Entry Level (Pretest)

Initial performance measures are more commonly known as "pretests." Unfortunately, pretests are often administered as a part of a school district's uniform testing program which requires that the results be immediately spirited away to repose in large master files which are examined only by statisticians. Absurd! Pretests should only be given in direct anticipation of a specific instructional objective, and then the results are of *immediate* importance only to the teacher. Having decided on a measure for the final performance, the pretest is used to discover how much of the final performance the student can already demonstrate. The pretest, or entry inventory, tells the teacher where to begin the shaping process so as to avoid the time-wasting tragedy (because it leads to boredom) of teaching things the student already knows.

Establish The Instructional Sequence

The steps between the pre- and posttest make up the instructional sequence. Consequently, an instructional sequence is a unit of arbitrary length. It is as long as the distance from the entry performance to the final performance. Depending on how the final performance is described, the instructional sequence may be a single lesson, a unit, a course, a text, or an entire curriculum.

If instructional sequences extend from one performance measure to the next, it follows that any measure of final performance can be used in a number of situations. Consider the process of evaluating the progress of a child through a learning sequence that has five units. If each unit has a measure of final performance called unit tests, then Unit Test 3 can be administered:

1. At the beginning of Unit 3 to determine how much of that unit the child already knows,

2. At the end of Unit 3 to determine if there are parts of the unit which need to be reemphasized for more complete mastery, and

3. At the end of Unit 3 to determine if the child has all the skills needed to begin Unit 4.

When Charlie's teacher used the fifteen-minute criterion the first time, she found an average of five minutes on-task — ten minutes short of her goal. Later, when Charlie reached the fifteen-minute criterion, he had reached the terminal performance for "attention span," *and* passed his pretest for beginning reading.

Most experienced teachers have always followed the practice of defining instructional objectives. The difference between their intuitive practice and Mager's is his insistence on clear measures. The difference is important.

TWO TYPES OF MEASUREMENT

Even though most teachers have found Mager's message attractive, they have frequently found it difficult to implement. The difficulty seems to come from the erroneous assumption that an instructional objective is a one-shot affair. Given this interpretation, the first-grade teacher would need to write a single set of objectives describing all the final performances of her students on the last school day of the year. Confronted by such a gigantic task, it is not surprising that the whole business of defining instructional objectives tends to be dismissed as "a nice idea, but not practical."

To make things more reasonable, let's divide the whole measurement business into two parts. One type of measure (the large one) can be left to professional test makers; the other type is the personal property of the classroom teacher.

Periodic Achievement Tests

Instruments which attempt to evaluate very large and complex instructional sequences (an entire grade level or more) are the familiar achievement tests which are standardized on very large populations of children. Prepared by specialists, these instruments are administered so they can provide information about how a child or a group of children of a given age compares with similar children throughout the nation in the skills which the instrument measures.

Standardized achievement tests such as the *Metropolitan Reading Readiness Test, Iowa Test of Basic Skills, Stanford Achievement Test,* and *Wide Range Achievement Test* can be useful in making administrative decisions. A curriculum supervisor, for example, might be interested in whether the children using reading curriculum *A* score better on a given test than children using curriculum *B.* Standardized achievement tests can also be useful in identifying gross weakness and outstanding skill in a general way. They provide a rough diagnosis of the educational health of a group of children. Just as the chart on a penny scale can indicate if you are over- or underweight for your height, these tests can indicate if the children in your class are over- or undereducated compared to other children of their age and grade. The difficulty is that they tell you nothing about *why* the results turn out as they do, nor do they suggest how to change the results on future occasions. Knowing you are underweight does not recommend a specific dietary change. Teachers need diagnostic instruments that suggest treatments.

Continuous Progress Measures

Achievement test results are usually not sensitive enough to provide recommendations for remediation, adjusted placement, the need for a specific kind of supplementary material, or an alternative instructional method. Lacking the ability to sharpen and improve teaching procedures, achievement tests can only serve to put labels on children and generate excuses not to teach. If, however, they are used along with other measures, the story can be very different.

A statement that the student will score 80 percent on the end-of-book test in math by the end of the year is somewhat better than an objective stated in terms of a standardized achievement test. Even though it limits attention to a single subject, it is still a pretty big bite to chew. By continuing to break the total objective into smaller and smaller units, more manageable objectives (approximations) are created, and the measurement process begins to make useful suggestions about the hows and whens of remediation, supplementary work, and the need for alternative teaching strategies.

Individual Progress Records. One of the most useful tools of the behavior analysis teacher is the Individual Progress Record.

Normally kept on a weekly basis, this record is constructed by breaking any major instructional objective into small, uniform segments. For example, if the completion of a standard text at the 80 percent mastery level is your objective, that text might be easily broken into mini-courses corresponding to the individual chapters of the book. A 200-page text that is to be completed in 40 weeks can be broken up as though it were 40 five-page booklets. Satisfactory completion of each five-page segment is the entry requirement for the next, and the instructional objective for a segment is far less intimidating than the global objectives attached to an entire book.

A simple and very useful chart can be drawn up which relates the smaller instructional sequences, or segments, to the amount of instructional time available. With a little practice, this chart can be a teacher's source of continuous and corrective feedback on entry level placement, progress, segments that are redundant, and segments that need supplements. It turns the notion of "defining instructional objectives" into a set of procedures which can be used to advantage in every classroom. Consider the amount of information provided by the chart in Figure 3-1.

This chart describes the progress of 6 children through the units of an arithmetic sequence over a 34-day period. The teacher has divided the entire sequence into 30 units which he judged to be of equivalent difficulty. At the end of each day's arithmetic lesson he put a slash by each child's name indicating the unit he was working on at the end of the day, or an *a* if the child was absent. For example, Alex Able took 3 days to complete Unit 1, and 3 days each for Units 2, 3, and 4. Units 5 and 6 took 6 days each; and then 7 and 8 were completed with only 2 days' work apiece. After 34 days of instruction, Alex was working in Unit 10, one-third of the way through the entire sequence.

Admittedly, such a chart is a few moments' extra work each day. Whether or not it is likely to be worth it depends on how much helpful information it can generate. What can you tell about the instructional sequence and about the six children by examining the sample progress record? By examining this record you can see that:

1. Mr. Sharp has really mastered the techniques of individualized instruction. Each child is progressing through the units independently without being dragged along or held back by the progress of other children.

INDIVIDUAL PROGRESS REPORT: ARITHMETIC

TEACHER: Mr. Sharp
GRADE: First

SCHOOL: Rose Garden
SEMESTER: Fall, 1971

	UNITS											
	1	2	3	4	5	6	7	8	9	10	11	12
ABLE, ALEX	III	III	III	IIα I	ℍL I	ℍL III	II	II	III	III		I
ACCURATE, ALICE	IIII	II	II	III	ℍL	ℍL II	II	I	II	III	III	
BOOMER, WM.	II	Iα I	II	IIII	ℍL II	ℍL I	II	II	IIα I	III	IIII	II
CAPABLE, CATHY	III	II	II	III	IIII	ℍL III	II	I	III	II	III	II
FAST, FRED	II	I	II	I	III	III	I	I	II	II	II	II
FAULTER, FRANK	ℍL	IIIα I	ℍL I	IIII	ℍLα ℍL	ℍL						

2. Units 1, 2, 3, and 4 appear to be well defined. Most of the children completed these initial units at the rate of about one every two or three days.

3. Units 5 and 6 of this sequence appear to be much more difficult than the first four. The next time around it would be advisable for Mr. Sharp to divide each of these units into two to provide a more certain sense of progress for the children.

4. Units 7 and 8, on the other hand, seem to be much less difficult than any of the preceding segments. All of the children (except Frank Faulter who will be discussed later) scooted through these segments in only a day or two.

5. Units 5 through 8 need to be redefined so they are somewhat more comparable in difficulty. Units that take too long to complete can put a heavy damper on a child's motivation and enthusiasm.

6. Frank Faulter needs special attention. The first obvious move is to recheck his pretest. His slow rate of progress should raise doubt over whether he has completely mastered the entry skills needed for this sequence. Since his progress is slow, it is also possible that he is not receiving adequate reinforcement for the work he is managing to get done. The combination of marginal background skills and a low rate of reinforcement will retard any child's progress to the point that the entire instructional sequence will become aversive. Unless immediate corrective steps are taken to get Frank moving through the units, there is good reason to expect him to present some behavior problems before very long.

7. Fred Fast's work also suggests that he may be in the wrong instructional sequence. In his case, however, his progress suggests that he already has the skills this sequence is trying to teach. By skipping him ahead to more advanced unit tests, the teacher can quickly learn where he belongs. Even though the nature of Fred's misplacement in the sequence is quite different from Frank's, the consequences may be very similar. If Fred can race through the material with very little effort, he will be able to maintain good progress and still have time to raise hell with Frank who has quit working because he's not getting anyplace.

It takes some study of the chart to pull useful information from it, but the advantages are reasonable compensation. Most important, the progress record provides exactly the kind of feedback to the teacher that helps refine and improve the structure and content of an instructional sequence each time it is used. Rather than shifting from one technique to another on the basis of fad or the latest cute idea from the teacher's lounge, changes can be based on data which progressively make the entire sequence more effective.

Class Progress Records. The Class Progress Record is a helpful first cousin to the Individual Progress Record. The Class Progress Record provides a one-glance summary of all the children's progress in a given subject. Although it does not provide quick information about an individual student, it can provide very helpful feedback to the teacher. The mechanics of constructing this kind of record are simple.

Figures 3–2 and 3–3 present the reading progress of two kindergarten classes. Thirty units of the reading sequence are arranged vertically along the left axis with the first unit at the bottom and the thirtieth at the top. The weeks of the school year are numbered from left to right along the bottom. At the end of each school week, these teachers have simply counted the number of children working in each unit and entered that number in the appropriate square. The result is a profile of the reading gains of each class. It is a single picture which conveys several messages.

First let's look at the record from Classroom A.

This teacher appears to be uncomfortable with the process of individualized instruction. Through the eighth week of the school year the entire class is very gradually moving through each unit at a standard pace. In the ninth week we can detect the first indication that the class is being broken into subgroups. The different rates of progress of the three groups which result is easily traced by examining the chart between weeks 15 and 25. The top group (Bluebirds) is progressing nicely at the rate of about one complete unit every two weeks. The Robins in the middle group are moving somewhat more slowly, and the bottom group of Vultures is slogging along at the rate of about four weeks per unit. Even though the three groups are moving at slightly different rates, every child within a given group is being advanced at the same rate as his fellows.

Finally, in the twenty-sixth week, the teacher begins to let the children in the top group break out at their own rates. It seems to have worked, because individualized progress for the middle group breaks out a short time later in week 31. For the last nine weeks of the school year, the teacher of this class has two-thirds of the

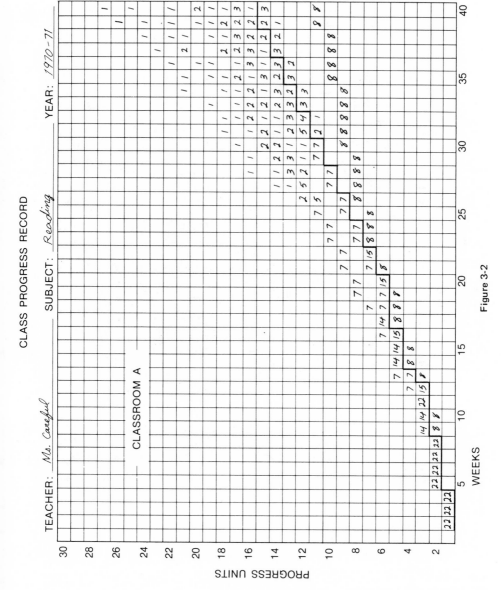

Figure 3-2

43

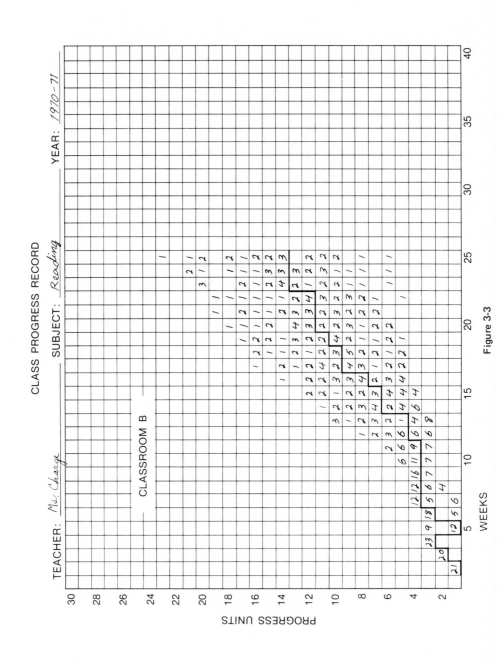

Figure 3-3

children engaged in individualized instruction. Unhappily, eight children are still inching forward at a common and slow pace.

The heavy line which has been added to the record locates the position of the median (middle) child in the class each week. The median line is a nice one-glance indicator of how things are going in a particular class. The steeper the slope, the faster the progress; and long flat plateaus are indications that something is hung up. For the teacher who has set targets for the year, the median line is also a handy way to keep track of whether or not the group is on course. It guards against that sudden realization that there are only four weeks left in the year and you are only halfway through the material you wanted to cover.

The rather close examination of the Class Progress Record of teacher A makes it easier to appreciate the excellence of teacher B. Rather than relying on a single one-shot pretest, teacher B ran the entire class through the first three units at a fairly rapid pace. By the end of week five she had decided that twelve of the children needed some careful review of initial concepts, so she backed them up while letting the rest of the class move ahead. By the eleventh week individualized placement is evident, and the amount of individualization increases steadily thereafter.

The slope of the median line is very encouraging, and the children have advanced as far in the 25 weeks of this record as the children in classroom A went in 36 weeks. Notice, however, the rate of progress of the faster children in both classes is about the same *once they are permitted to move at their own individual rates.* Clearly, classroom B did not have more "bright" children. The big difference in the general progress of these two classes is in the progress of the slower third of each class.

In classroom A, the teacher kept eight children in the slow group moving together on the apparent assumption that all of them needed the same instructional experience. That assumption is always wrong. In this case it is reasonable to guess that four or five of the children in that group were held back by the teacher's preoccupation with the special needs of two or three children.

Teacher B (our heroine) applied individualized teaching techniques to all of the children in such a way that she was able to devote extra personal attention to those few children who needed it while the other children continued to move ahead.

The teacher who constructs, and learns to read, Individual and Class Progress Records can continuously improve her own teaching by adjusting her practices according to the effects shown by such records. When a unit or a particular teaching strategy doesn't produce the results hoped for, the fact is obvious and appropriate corrective action can be taken. When things go well, it is equally obvious, and being able to record substantial progress is likely to reinforce the use of more effective techniques.

Personal Progress Records (report cards). Some schools are now using progress records instead of the old-style report card. The Personal Progress Record also contains the bottom to top arrangement of units along the vertical axis, but only ten time divisions are made along the bottom of this chart — one for each month of the school year.

Figure 3-4

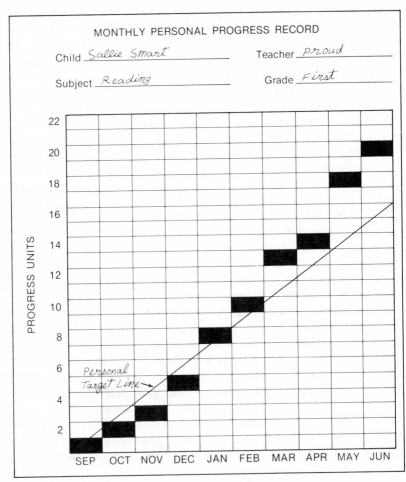

Each month a child takes his Personal Progress Record home to be signed and returned. Each month, the child's parents are able to see where he is working; how much progress he has made since last month; and how much progress he has made since the beginning of the year. A simple chart like Figure 3-4 for each subject which has a well defined instructional sequence is a great advance over the reports which describe a child's proficiency in terms of plus and minus or *S* and *U*.

REFERENCE

Mager, Robert F., *Preparing Instructional Objectives.* Belmont, Calif.: Fearon Publishers, 1962.

4

Learning is
a Participant Sport

*Yet, withal, the teacher
constitutes the principal aid in
the teaching process as it is
practiced in our schools.*

Jerome S. Bruner, 1961

The message of this chapter is very direct: effective teaching can best occur when students engage in large amounts of behavior. A child does not learn to skate by watching; neither does a student learn to read or write by observing others. We can listen to people converse in Russian or Latin, but we begin to learn a language as we utter approximate sounds which are differentially attended to (reinforced) by a listener. Since it is only by behaving that children put themselves in a position to experience reinforcement, a major function of the classroom environment is to prompt large amounts of behavior.

Remembering that a learning episode consists of a prompt, a behavior, and a consequence, the whole issue can be summarized by:

Rule: The effectiveness of any learning situation is proportional to the number of learning episodes it generates.

Lavishly decorated classrooms, where the bulletin boards are changed every week and brightly colored mobiles hang from every square of accoustical tile, are often thought to be effective classrooms. Rubbish! Or at least that is what all the decorations might as well be if they are not used to prompt specific behaviors from the children. A rather sparsely furnished classroom can be just as effective, or more so, if every element in the room is used to engage the children in action. The various strategies which can be used to prompt more and better approximations need special consideration.

GETTING MORE BEHAVIOR TO REINFORCE: PROMPTING

There are all sorts of things that teachers do to prompt appropriate classroom behavior. A well-selected question prompts an answer, a well-formulated problem prompts a solution, and a properly delivered instruction prompts performance. Each of these examples stresses the importance of selecting the correct prompting strategy for each situation. Repeating a question that was not successful in prompting an answer the first time, is not likely to be any more effective the second time. Instead of badgering the child, a skillful teacher responds to silence by shifting to a prompt that will increase the probability of an answer, or a reasonable approximation of an answer. Once the child has responded in some way you at least have a behavior to shape on. Without the child's behavior, you have nothing to work with.

The objective is to use prompts that are most likely to get an appropriate response. Prompts that elicit incorrect or irrelevant responses delay the reinforcement needed to keep the sequence moving. The prompting strategy that maximizes responding and minimizes errors is particularly handy.

Using A Familiar Prompt To Develop A New One —
Fading

If you point to a four-legged, furry animal that is barking loudly as he chases his own tail and ask a three-year-old, "What is that?" he will answer, "dog!" If you show that same child a card bearing the letters D-O-G and ask, "What is this?" the best you can usually hope for is the reply, "sign." At this point the printed word DOG is not an effective prompt for the child to say "dog." The actual dog is, however, so you know that the child is capable of making the correct response given the right prompts. At some future date, a teacher will have the job of insuring that DOG prompts the verbal response "dog," just as accurately as the animal itself. The appropriate behavior is already present. The task is to make a new event (a printed word) an effective prompt for the old behavior. The process is called fading. When a behavior that is under the control of one prompt comes under the control of a new prompt, fading has occurred.

Without technical knowledge of the fading process, most kindergarten teachers nevertheless use it to teach color names.

Teacher: (Holding up a solid color paper circle) What color is this, Tom?

Tom: (no answer)

Teacher: This is green, Tom. Can you say green?

Tom: Green.

Teacher: That's right, green. What color is this?

Tom: Green.

In this sequence the answer "green" is initially prompted by the teacher's statement, "Can you say green?" Once the correct statement has been made, subsequent steps can be used to fade the control of "green" to a colored paper circle. The pattern is always the same in a fading sequence:

1. In the presence of the new prompt, use the familiar prompt to encourage a behavior.

2. When the appropriate behavior occurs, reinforce it immediately.

3. Gradually, use progressively more of the new prompt and less of the original prompt.

4. Reinforce each correct response, immediately.

The more gradually the transition is made from the old to the new prompt, the greater the chances that the behavior will be correct. The more often the behavior is reinforced in the presence of the new prompt, the more quickly the new prompt will become effective.

Fading has been used to teach very young preschool children to correctly match a numeral with the appropriate number of dots. The children first learned to pick out the one square of three which showed the same number of dots as shown in a sample picture (see Figure 4-1a). Each time they picked the picture which matched the sample they were immediately reinforced.

Figure 4-1a

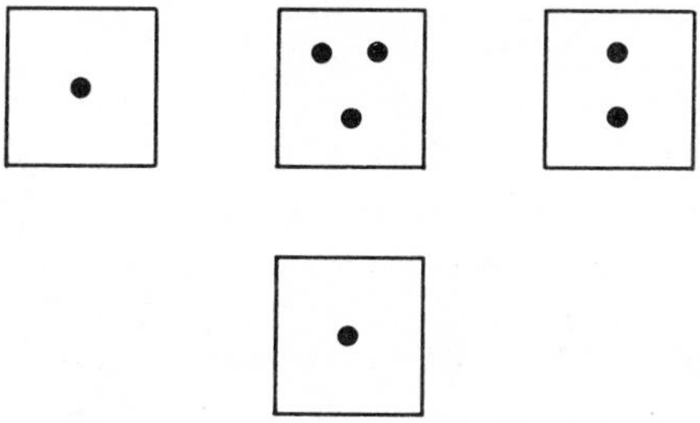

There was opportunity after opportunity to match samples. Then, slowly, an interesting thing began to happen. The sample dot began to appear superimposed on a very faint numeral one. Almost unnoticeable at first, the numeral soon became quite prominent and the dot was less and less apparent (see Figure 4-1b).

Figure 4-1b

Throughout many successive trials, the children continued to push the lower panel which displayed a single dot even though the sample looked less and less like a dot and more and more like the numeral 1. Through even later trials, a two-dot pattern slowly became a numeral 2, a three-dot pattern became a 3, etc. (see Figure 4-1c). The matching behavior, originally prompted by identical images, was faded to the control of symbols which represented the number of dots in the picture.

Figure 4-1c

Even though the dot-fading technique may be more valuable as a research procedure than as a general classroom strategy, it depends on exactly the same principle that was illustrated when the teacher said "green" while holding up a green circle. Pictures fade from children's readers as printed words develop stronger and stronger control over responding. The need for spoken instructions fades as the pattern of the daily schedule prompts smooth transitions from one activity to another.

When the fade from one prompt to another is too abrupt, control is lost, and the sequence breaks down. It is a common error, but easy to correct. The process can quickly be restarted by simply dropping back to a greater reliance on the original prompt and fade in the new one more slowly. A very large proportion of the instructional objectives of the primary grades involves teaching children to make familiar responses to new kinds of prompts. In every one of these cases, fading can be a powerful strategy.

A delightful example of fading is provided by a note in *The Reader's Digest.*[1] The gradual transition of orthographics is elegantly described by M. J. Shields (Yilz). Notice how difficult it would be to read the last paragraph without going through the entire fading sequence.

Man of Letters

In a letter to *The Economist,* M. J. Shields, of Jarrow, England, points out that George Bernard Shaw, among others, urged spelling reform, suggesting that one letter be altered or deleted each year, thus giving the populace time to absorb the change. Shields writes:

For example, in Year 1 that useless letter "c" would be dropped to be replased by either "k" or "s," and likewise "x" would no longer be part of the alphabet. The only kase in which "c" would be retained would be the "ch" formation, which will be dealt with later. Year 2 might well reform "w" spelling, so that "which" and "one" would take the same konsonant, wile Year 3 might well abolish "y" replasing it with "i," and lear 4 might fiks the "g-j" anomali wonse and for all.

Jenerally, then, the improvement would kontinue iear bai iear, with lear 5 doing awai with useless double konsonants, and lears 6-12 or so modifaiing vowlz and the rimeining voist and unvoist konsonants. Bai ler 15 or sou, it wud fainali bi posibl tu meik ius ov thi ridandant letez "c," "y" and "x" — bai now jast a memori in the maindz ov ould doderez — tu riplais "ch," "sh" and "th" rispektivli.

Fainali, xen, aafte sam 20 iers ov orxogrefkl riform, wi wud hev a lojikl, kohirnt speling in ius xrewawt xe Ingliy-spiking werld. Haweve, sins xe Wely, xe Airiy, and xe Skots du not spik Ingliy, xei wud hev to hev a speling siutd tu xer oun lengwij. Xei kud, haweve, orlweiz lern Ingliy az a sekond lengwij et skuul! — Iorz feixfuli, M. J. Yilz.

Combining Fading With Shaping

The film, *Behavior Theory In Practice* (Reese, 1965), contains a scene in which a pigeon is in a plexiglas cage and a sign saying PECK appears in a window on one of the walls. The pigeon moves to the sign and pecks it with his beak. The sign then changes to TURN and the pigeon turns around in a full circle. The PECK sign reappears, and again the pigeon walks over and pecks the sign. Since reading skill is judged by the degree to which a person's

[1] M. J. Shields' letter is reprinted as it appeared in *The Reader's Digest,* July 1971, with the permission of *The Economist.*

behavior (verbal or nonverbal) is correctly prompted by different printed symbols, it could be argued that the pigeon was "reading." Rather than debating whether or not the bird was really reading, however, let's examine the instructional process used to develop this kind of behavior.

The pigeon's training involved both shaping and fading and was done by two undergraduates taking their first laboratory course in psychology from Dr. Ellen P. Reese (1966) at Mount Holyoke College. She reports that it took them less than an hour to teach the bird to respond differently to each of these two words.

> Initially, the bird was taught, by shaping, to peck a black circle on the front of the chamber. By providing a small amount of food as reinforcement each time the pigeon's head bobbed closer (a better approximation) to the circle, pecking the black circle was soon established. Next, they presented the word PECK, printed in black where the circle had been and the behavior of pecking black things in the window generalized — the bird pecked the black letters and was immediately reinforced.
>
> Next, discrimination training was begun. The word TURN was presented in red letters and pecking this sign was never reinforced. The red TURN and the black PECK were presented in random order, but pecking was reinforced only in the presence of the word PECK. When TURN appeared, each approximation of turning in a circle was reinforced. "First, reinforcement was presented when the bird turned his head toward the right wall of the chamber. Then reinforcement was withheld until he turned his body. Gradually, closer approximations to turning a full circle were required: lifting his foot, moving both feet a quarter turn, moving a half turn, and so forth." At the end of this shaping sequence, the bird would turn a full circle when TURN appeared and he would peck when PECK appeared. Both words were still being presented in random order.
>
> The final step required that the red letters in TURN be gradually faded darker until they were black. Initially, the turning behavior was prompted by the color red. At the end of the fading process, the same behavior was controlled by a black TURN. The distinctive shape of the word TURN rather than its color had become the effective prompt.

Clearly, combining fading (altering the form of the prompt) with shaping (reinforcing improvements) is a very powerful educational strategy. The gradually changing prompt maintains a high rate of behavior which maximizes the opportunity for reinforcement. Theoretically, it might be possible to use shaping alone to change behavior, but as a practical matter there is almost always some form of prompt used to increase the chances of improvement.

Using One Behavior To Prompt Another — Chaining

Another strategy which is often used to prompt greater amounts of correct student behavior is called chaining. Technically, a behavioral chain exists when one behavior produces the prompt for the next. Walking, counting, reciting the alphabet or a poem, or learning to play a piano piece from memory all illustrate the development of behavioral chains.

Counting, the recitation of "one," "two," "three," etc., can be used as an example. Normally, you teach a child to count by saying something like, "Count to ten for me. One . . ." If the counting chain is fairly well established, your spoken "one" will be a sufficient prompt for the child to say, "one, two, three," and so on to "ten." In this sequence, the sound of the world "one" is the prompt for the word "two." The sound of the word "two" is the prompt for the word "three," and so on through the higher numbers. There are still three elements present in the learning episode (prompt, behavior, and consequence), but in a chain, the consequence of one behavior is also the prompt for the next. The consequence of saying "one" is hearing the sound, "one"; and hearing the sound "one" is the prompt for saying "two."

To appreciate how strong the links of a behavior chain are you need only ask a child to count to ten for you and start him at "seven." So many of the early links are missing, only very experienced counters can pick up the chain in mid-sentence. Chaining is not restricted to children. The strength of the alphabet chain is demonstrated each time most of us pick up a dictionary or a phone book to look for a word or a name. To get our bearings, we usually have to run off several links of the "a-b-c" chain. You can convince yourself that reciting the alphabet is a strong behavior chain by trying to recite backwards from z. Every letter is a strong prompt for the one which follows it, but not for the one before it. Each time you hear yourself say "p" it prompts "q" rather than "o."

How many days in October? You probably have to recite some portion of the chain, "Thirty days hath September, April, June, and November, etc.," to come up with the answer. If you play the piano, what happens when you have to stop in the middle of a piece you are memorizing? Unless it is very thoroughly memorized, you probably have to start again at the beginning and go through the entire chain. The chain is very fragile in the early stages and you need every prompt (link) in just the right sequence to make it all the way through. Once the chain begins to take shape, however, it is a very efficient way to prompt large amounts of correct behavior. Indeed, without this kind of behavioral patterning, life would consist of such an endless number of trivial decisions that it would take until noon to complete the daily routine of getting up, dressing, and arriving at work. Remember the teacher mentioned earlier who made the end of the morning song the prompt for beginning a reading lesson? She was building a patterned schedule for the school day so that the end of each activity was the signal for the next. Without this kind of chain, the whole day would be devoted to transitions between activities and there would be little time left for actual instruction.

Building A Behavioral Chain

Constant repetition is not enough. Saying something over and over again in the presence of a child will not teach him to say it. Even having him say it over and over with you will not guarantee results. Behavioral chains, just like other behaviors, are strengthened (learned) by well-timed reinforcement. In a chain the strongest and most important reinforcer is the one that comes at the end of the sequence. For this reason it is usually the links toward the end of the chain (closest to the reinforcer) that are mastered first. If you've watched a child learn to count to 10 or say the alphabet you've seen the final steps of 8, 9, 10 or x, y, z said with greater speed and assurance than those in the middle of the chain. This pattern is so regular in chained sequences it suggests a strategy for teaching.

Rule: Most behavioral chains are easiest to teach by starting at the end and working toward the beginning.

Example 1. Following the rule, a piano student should memorize a short piece by first learning to play it correctly while looking at the music. The next step would be to follow the music all the way except for the last measure. The next would be to look away for the last *two* measures, and so on. While reading the music, the pianist has at least three prompts controlling the sequence of his finger movements: the notes printed on the page, the kinesthetic feedback (muscle movement), and the pattern of sounds. By gradually removing the printed notes from the end of the sequence, the other two prompts become progressively stronger.

Example 2. The rule also suggests a way to teach a child to count to ten. First, get the child to count along with you as you recite, "One, two, three, . . . ten." At the end of the sequence when you and the child have mastered the chain in unison, great praise and excitement should prevail. "You did it, Andy! You're learning how to count! Beautiful! Do you want to do it again?" Assuming your jubilant praise is a reinforcer, Andy will want to do it again, and you're ready for the next step. This time the two of you count together through "nine," but you just shape your mouth to say "ten" without actually making a sound. If the pace of your unison counting is reasonably smooth, Andy is going to say ten even if you don't. Now you are really set up for a party, *because he did it all by himself!* From here on, successive recitations of the chain will contain progressively more of Andy by himself and less of you as a prompter.

As was mentioned earlier, chains can be rather fragile in the beginning. It would not be unusual for you to find that Andy's counting chain broke down as you tried to drop your prompt from "five" back to "four." When this happens all you have to do is increase your prompting again for a few times (maybe back up to "six") and then gradually start down again. Don't be stingy with your praise. If "five" has been a stumbling point, slip an extra "That's right," into the middle of the sequence.

Example 3. The rule also suggests that most of us learned long division the hard way rather than the easy way. The entire process still seems like an unsystematic guessing game.

$$\text{Divide:}\quad 123\,\overline{\smash{\big)}\,52767}$$

The only prompt I can remember went something like, "How many times will 123 go into 527?" I then learned, by working it out, that 5 was too many and 3 wasn't enough. By this time the original numbers were almost completely erased away and the whole encounter was becoming distinctly unpleasant (nonreinforcing). Consider the possibility of setting up a sequence to teach long division that followed the rule of building a chain by working backward.

$$
\begin{array}{r}
429 \\
123\overline{)52767} \\
492 \\
356 \\
246 \\
1107 \\
\hline
\end{array}
$$

Finish the problem:

The first step in this sequence is to prompt the student through each of the moves that bring the problem to this stage (4 × 123 = 492; subtract 492 from 527; bring down the 6; etc.). To complete the solution, the student only has to multiply 9× 123, enter the 1107, and have his work confirmed. Successive steps would require progressively more of the solution, but each would allow for a repetition of familiar moves — moves that had previously been reinforced. With an increase in reinforcement and a decrease in erasures, the process should be as much easier to teach as it would be to learn.

SELECTING A GOOD CURRICULUM

In any elementary classroom most of the children's learning behaviors are supposed to be prompted by the books and instructional materials that define the curriculum. The use of a particular textbook series is likely to have a stronger influence on the shape and form of an instructional sequence than anything else. In spite of its importance, however, the adoption of a particular set of materials often depends on some very strange factors. A selection committee decides to adopt a particular reading series because one of their group studied with the author in college and thought "He was just wonderful." An elementary mathematics series is adopted because that publisher's representative made a smoother presentation than his competitors. A language arts series is selected because it has better pictures. Seldom, if ever, has a curriculum series been adopted because it taught better.

It's hard to imagine that every set of materials is just as effective as any other, and it's also hard to imagine that the curriculum is so unimportant it doesn't really matter. Perhaps the increasing importance of performance contracting in education will stimulate some changes, but as things stand now, schools are not in a good position to select curriculums on the basis of their proven effectiveness. One of the reasons for this difficulty is that the schools have not established a reasonable set of criteria for evaluating curriculum materials. For the moment, let's leave aside the question of how well children learn from the materials. As a first step we need only ask whether the materials are constructed to meet the requirements of good teaching.

By combining the requirements for defining and measuring instructional objectives with the requirements of a favorable learning situation, a set of rules can be developed for evaluating curriculums. Each rule can be put in the form of a question to be asked about the book, series, or course outline in question. The more clearly the answer to each question is "yes," the better. Since an instructional sequence may be a single lesson, a unit of several lessons, a text, or an entire series of texts, the word curriculum is a handy way to refer to any sequence.

Does The Curriculum Describe The Terminal Behavior?

A lot of texts do reasonably well in defining their objectives. The most common practice is to state the objective by including an end-of-book test in the teacher's manual or an accompanying test booklet. It may not seem elegant or esthetically pleasing, but at least that final test gives you some specific referent for deciding if the author of the text has the same objectives in mind that you have. If the curriculum does not contain some final checkout procedure, give it a low mark on the first criterion.

Does The Curriculum Measure The Student's Entry Level?

Unless an instructional sequence provides for the identification of the different entering skills which students bring to it, the teacher is faced with a long period of guessing, trying, backing, patching, guessing and trying again. The job will eventually get done, and the teacher will come to know what each child needs. The guessing and trying process is costly and slow, however, when compared to the easy flow of information from a well-designed entry test. The sooner a teacher can correctly identify entry skills, the sooner improvements can be accurately detected and reinforced. Lacking that information makes it impossible to provide well-timed differential reinforcement for student progress. There is simply no way of knowing what progress is. When evaluating curriculums, give your high marks to the ones with well-constructed inventories or placement tests.

Does The Curriculum Require Frequent Student Responding?

It has already been established that the most effective learning situation is the one that generates the most learning episodes. It is also true that the most effective curriculum is the one that prompts the most behavior. The more often the student responds, the more often improvements can be reinforced to speed the learning process. This means, of course, that the responses need to be public and observable. Private unobserved behaviors can't count because a teacher has no way of knowing when to reinforce them. Another refinement in this criterion is to count only those responses which leave some sort of physical trace or evidence. Marks on a piece of paper, paint on a canvas, a tape recording, or a written report are all familiar ways of documenting the fact that a student has made some response to the prompts of the curriculum. These records of student behavior are permanent enough to allow a teacher to deliver reinforcement and correction without having to hover over each child as he works. When comparing the probable advantages of two curriculums, give your highest marks to the one which requires the largest number of student responses that will leave observable traces.

Does The Curriculum Contain Clear Criteria For Correct Responses?

Unless a curriculum sequence is quite specific about what constitutes a correct response, it is not possible to reinforce an improvement. If a curriculum has a clearly stated terminal objective then each required response should be a step toward that objective. If there is any ambiguity about what kind of response is most appropriate, the teacher has no clear way of knowing when or what to reinforce. This does not say that open-ended or undefined response opportunities are bad. It does emphasize, once again, the importance of being able to recognize and differentially reinforce students' progress.

Does The Curriculum Contain Check Points and Prescriptions?

Current education jargon includes the phrase, "curriculum imbedded test." It's a fancy label, but the idea is as familiar as the end-of-chapter quizzes we all grew up with. Any instructional sequence needs to contain periodic check points which allow the student to demonstrate that he has mastered the material just presented. These checks need to be frequent enough that any difficulty can be spotted before it becomes too serious. Further, the results of the check need to suggest what the next unit in the sequence should be for a student. Do the results lead the teacher to prescribe that the child drop back and repeat the last unit, or do they recommend that the child be skipped ahead to more advanced work? Any curriculum needs to be designed so that it provides clear feedback to the teacher. The curriculum that actually does so deserves high marks on the evaluation.

Does The Curriculum Accommodate Individual Differences?

Everybody talks about individual differences, but only a few have done anything about them. Most curriculums still require that every child in a group progress at the same rate. Even if a class has three subgroups, within each of them the rate of progress is going to be too slow for some, too fast for others, and just right for only a very few. Too many teachers feel as though they are teaching only when they are giving a lesson to the entire class even though they admit that some don't need to hear it, some aren't prepared to understand it, and only a few are likely to profit from the session.

There is the mistaken notion that individualized instruction must be programmed (frame by frame) instruction. This is not true; programmed materials certainly do have some great advantages, but nonprogrammed curriculums can be designed for individual rates of progress. One of the best examples of this that I have seen was designed by a teacher in a rural school in Montana. Her strategy was to break an entire reading curriculum (one that assumed whole-class presentations) into small units. For each unit she then prepared a little booklet of instructions and check points. Each child in the class had his own booklet and was able to follow its instructions at his own rate. The check points in the booklets allowed the teacher to monitor the progress of each individual child. A sample of this teacher's ingenious procedure illustrates the technique.

Sample[2]

Turn to page 318 in your reading book. There is a word list there of the new words on each page of your reader. Study the words for pages 45, 46, 47, 48, 49, and 50. If you have trouble with some of them, hold up your hand for a teacher to help you. When you can say all of them, pronounce them to a teacher. She must give you an OK and write her initials in the little box here, before you go on to the next part.

Word List, pp. 45-50 . . . . ☐☐

Now turn to the reading part of your book and study the story from pages 46 to 50. Try to read it to yourself at least three times, so you can read all the words and tell about the people and things that happened in the story. Your teacher will ask you some questions about it and pick out one page for you to read aloud. When you can answer the questions and read well enough to suit her, she will give you an OK and write her initials in this little box.

Questions and Oral Reading . . . . ☐☐

Now get your workbook and work on page 8, Part 1 of your workbook. Take your time and think, because we want you to get a good grade on this. Then put your name on both sides of the page and hand it in to [the teacher]. She will give you an OK and write her initials in the little box.

Workbook, Part 1, p. 8 . . . . ☐☐

When you get this paper back with your grade on it, you can fill in the graph at the end of this little book that we will tell you about.

Next turn to Part 2, page 8. Read the questions and answer each one with a complete sentence the way it shows you in Question 1. You will

[2] Adapted with the kind permission of Mrs. Josephine Thex, Behavior Analysis Follow Through teacher in the Primary Center, St. Labre Mission School, Ashland, Montana.

need the words at the top of the page to write your answers. These words have consonant digraphs in them. There are four digraphs:

> kn — sounds n.　　The k is silent.
> wr — sounds r.　　The w is silent.
> ph — sounds f.
> gh — sounds f.

Underline words with these digraphs in them in the sentences you write. Be sure you do all you are supposed to do on this page. Look it over before you hand it in. Write your name on it. Then tear it out and take it to [the teacher] for her OK and initials.

> Workbook, Part 2, p. 8 . . . . ☐☐

When you get it back, you may have to do part of it over before you can fill in the graph for the page. Get an OK from a teacher.

Study the vocabulary from page 66 to page 69 on page 319. Say them and talk about them to a teacher and get her OK.

> Word List, pp. 66-69 . . . . ☐☐

Study your story and have a teacher ask you questions and listen to you read and get her OK.

> Questions and Oral Reading . . . . ☐☐

Work on page 12 in Part 1 of your workbook. In each part there are two words to pick from. Only one will work in *both* sentences of each part, so think while you do this. Put your name on the page, tear it out, and take it to [the teacher] for her OK.

> Workbook, Part 1, page 12 . . . . ☐☐
> Workbook, Part 1, page 12 reviewed and recorded . ☐☐

Now turn to Part 2 of your workbook and work on page 12. It is tricky, but read the directions and be careful. Write your name on it, tear it out, and take it to [the teacher].

> Workbook, Part 2, page 12 . . . . ☐☐
> Workbook, Part 2, page 12 reviewed and recorded . . ☐☐

Match these words by writing the number of each word in List 1 by the word in List 2 that means the opposite.

List 1		List 2
1. angry	_____	friend
2. women	_____	begin
3. shout	_____	glad
4. enemy	_____	slowly
5. quickly	_____	men
6. end	_____	whisper

Underline all the words in these sentences that have a long *o* sound.

I will phone the store for a loaf of bread.

Father drove home on the new road.

We have no more rope.

Those roses are very pretty.

Joe's mother boasted about the note he wrote.

Exercises, completed. . . . . ☐☐

The curriculum sequence this teacher was working with would score rather badly on all six of the selection criteria mentioned below. With the addition of the teacher's study booklets, however, the curriculum rates high on every count. Given its obvious advantages, one has to wonder why the authors and publishers of that curriculum didn't include similar procedures initially. The point is rhetorical; the authors and publishers of curriculums are not likely to improve their product until their consumers establish higher criteria. Hopefully, those discussed in this chapter provide a step in the right direction.

Elements of an Instructional Sequence

1. Describes the behavior the student will be capable of at the end of the sequence.

2. Measures the student's entering skills.

3. Requires frequent responding by the student.

4. Contains clear criteria for a "correct" response.

5. Provides for periodic testing of progress.

6. Allows for individual rates of progress.

REFERENCES

Reese, Ellen P., *Behavior Theory in Practice.* Filmed by Charter Oak Studios, New York: Appleton-Century-Crofts, 1965.

————, "The analysis of human operant behavior," in J. Vernon (ed.), *Introduction to Psychology: A Self-Selection Text-book.* Dubuque, Iowa: Wm. C. Brown Company, 1966.

The Reader's Digest, "Man of Letters." Pleasantville, New York: July, 1971, p. 128.

5

Eliminating

Problem Behavior

"*. . . education ought to be carried on with a severe sweetness, quite contrary to the practice of our pedants, who, instead of tempting and alluring children to letters by apt and gentle ways, do in truth present nothing before them but rods and ferules, horror and cruelty. Away with this violence! Away with this compulsion!*"

Montaigne, 1580

In fact, this chapter is an extension of the former, for it too is concerned with creating a favorable learning situation. A skilled teacher must be as effective in minimizing problem behavior as in maximizing the frequency of appropriate behavior. Even though many have cautioned teachers against the use of punishment to control undesirable classroom behavior, fewer have suggested practical alternatives. Now there are alternatives.

Research conducted during the last ten years has produced a whole new body of information about the effects of coercion and punishment on learning. In sum, this new information makes it clear that punitive control is incompatible with good teaching. Consequently, behavior analysis teachers seek the elimination of all harsh punishment and coercion from their classrooms. The position is not a moral one; it is pragmatic. There are other procedures which are far superior.

WHY NOT PUNISH?

In a classroom where positive reinforcement is the rule, the teacher and all she is associated with soon become reinforcing. Things are very different, however, if the teacher is a source of *both* reinforcement and punishment. A teacher who has often punished a child may reach toward him intending to deliver an encouraging pat for good performance; however, if past experience has made that teacher's attention ambiguous (sometimes reinforcing, sometimes punitive) the child might flinch away from the touch, thinking it the prologue to a slap. What the teacher intends as a reinforcer turns out to be a threat, and the opportunity to strengthen an appropriate behavior is lost.

Rule: The reinforcing value of a teacher's attention is reduced to the extent that he is a source of punishment.

71

Punishing A Bad Behavior Does Not Teach A Good
Behavior

Punishment also suffers bad marks because it is a very inefficient way to teach. The teacher who wants a child to read a book can encourage it with lots of reinforcement for approximations, by suggestion, by making a game of it, *or* by punishing anything else the child tries to do. All of these approaches might be expected to work sooner or later, but the punishment strategy will work later and will be the most difficult for everyone involved. If you imagine that all the behaviors a child might engage in are represented by the 360 points on the face of a compass, you can decide whether to reinforce the one behavior you want, or punish away all of the 359 others. Does this seem too extreme? How often are children put into situations where only punishment can result because they have not learned how to perform the behavior that will result in reinforcement? A child who is deficient in math has little opportunity to contact the reinforcers available in science, and a fifth grader who cannot read is cut off from most of the reinforcers the school has to offer.

Punishment Effects Generalize

Punishment is likely to be sloppy in its effects. Unfortunately, when a teacher scolds or abuses a child in the classroom it does not affect an isolated undesirable behavior. Soon, the teacher (who needs to be an effective reinforcer), the subject matter, the room, even the building, all become associated with punishment. The result is sometimes called anxiety. Whatever the name, and regardless of whether it is experienced as mild uneasiness or physical illness, it reduces the amount of behavior the child will exhibit. We've already emphasized the importance of getting large amounts of behavior out of students, and now it turns out that some rather common school practices have just the opposite effect.

Avoidance

Any rational person is going to do his best to avoid unpleasant situations. Children are rational people. In your own experience, who are the ones that are tardy the most often? Who tends to be the last one in from recess? Who always has another pencil to sharpen or question to ask before getting on with it? A mildly aversive situation or an assignment will be greeted with gentle forms of avoidance, but since these ploys often generate more of the punishment they were meant to avoid, the process escalates. The child who is punished for his tardiness soon learns that it is better to be absent entirely than to arrive late, and is often stricken with early morning stomach aches.

Escape

More than anything else, the exuberance which children display as they burst from school on the last day before vacation suggests that they are escaping from a very unpleasant situation. The way to test the reinforcing value of any situation is to provide an alternative and observe the choices that people will make. Following this rule let's arrange a situation so that children can choose whether or not they will remain in school. Do you count among your friends a large number who resent the way recess intrudes upon their study? Have you read lately about students protesting because there were too many vacations? So long as our schools continue to rely on commands, coercion, threats, and actual punishment, any opportunity to escape the setting will be welcomed by the student.

Most of us have learned to escape from unpleasant or nonreinforcing situations with great civility. We daydream — a mild form of escape which allows us to transport ourselves beyond the constraints of a mildly aversive situation. Increased coercion, however, amplifies escape behavior. In a school situation it takes skill — academic and social skill — to come into contact with the reinforcers the system has to offer students. Children who lack those skills are set up to contact more punishment and less reinforcement through each month they spend in the system. There is nothing mysterious about school dropouts!

Aggression

During the 1967-1968 school year New York City spent 1.21 million dollars to replace broken windows. In that same year, the city of Chicago put a price tag of nearly 2 million dollars on school vandalism. That amount could have paid the first year salaries of two hundred beginning teachers, but it didn't. Instead nearly half of the total went to glass companies and maintenance men. In school districts throughout the country, the physical evidence of assaults on schools is mounting. Some observers have told us that it is the reaction of the young against the establishment and against authority. If that is the case, why don't we hear about the broken windows of other establishment buildings such as churches, factories, car dealers, hospitals, city halls, and libraries? Could it be explained by the different amounts of punishment that people have experienced in these settings? Remember, the entire setting where punishment occurs tends to become aversive.

Most of us submitted to the coercive practices of our school with varying degrees of gracefulness. We encountered success and reinforcement often enough to make school a reasonably enjoyable experience. Many of our contemporaries, however, knew twelve or more years of relative discomfort in the school situation. Now they have a very civil, but a very destructive, way to aggress against the schools in which they knew so little reinforcement. They vote down bond issues and reject school levies.

If they are passed in review, the answers to the question, "Why not punish?" make a formidable list.

Punishment

1. Reduces the reinforcing value of the teacher's attention,

2. Is an inefficient way to teach new behaviors,

3. Can generalize to make an entire setting aversive,

4. Increases avoidance behaviors,

5. Promotes a variety of escape attempts, and

6. Generates aggressive reactions.

A BEHAVIORAL REASON FOR PUNISHMENT

In spite of the above liabilities, it is possible to witness all kinds of coercion and punishment being used in schools every day of the week. Why is punishment so prevalent? The answer is probably very simple. Punishment reinforces the punisher!

The typical occasion for punishment involves some behavior which annoys or is upsetting to a teacher. Doing something which gets rid of the annoyance is very reinforcing. A technique which appears to be immediately effective will be used more often in the future. Ironically, when a child is threatened because of his misconduct and he straightens up, his momentary obedience has the effect of reinforcing threats. Children teach teachers to punish!

Children can reinforce a teacher's abusiveness in diabolical ways. One recent study (Madsen et al., 1968) clearly showed that the more often first grade teachers told their students to sit down, the more often they stood up! When a child got out of his seat, the teacher would say, "Sit down." Reinforced by the instant success of her command, the teacher was more likely to repeat the process. To make matters worse, the attention she provided as she said "sit down" proved to be a reinforcer to the children. Now you have the unpleasant picture. The teacher's "sit down" commands were reinforced by the children's obedience; and the children's standing up was increased by the attention of the teacher's commands.

So that we don't leave those first graders bobbing up and down, it should be reported that Madsen and his colleagues eliminated standing up by praising the children when they were seated. Indeed that bit of information introduces an entirely different approach to the elimination of undesirable classroom behavior.

DISCIPLINE: ANOTHER POINT OF VIEW

What we need at this point is a new definition of classroom discipline. *Discipline is a set of procedures designed to eliminate behaviors that compete with effective learning.* The value of this definition is that it emphasizes the importance of *simultaneously* dealing with learning and with any behaviors that conflict with learning. For the pragmatist it is not difficult to recognize that the best way to reduce one practice is to offer an alternative that has superior outcomes.

There are some very straightforward, basic procedures for altering behavior in such a way that undesirable or problem behaviors are eliminated and desirable behaviors are strengthened. Although the preceding discussion of punishment considered only one side of the issue (the punishment of the undesirable behavior), the following strategies will always deal with different consequences for two types of behaviors. Effective discipline procedures arrange for consequences which reduce undesirable behavior, while, at the same time, they provide strong and consistent reinforcement for appropriate behaviors.

Children cannot talk and be silent at the same time. They are not cooperative with each other and fighting simultaneously. They do not study as they gaze out of the window. They do not recite to the teacher while they are talking to their fellows. The best way to reduce the frequency of an undesirable behavior is to teach, with reinforcement, the opposite (incompatible) behavior. It is an obvious strategy, but one too often neglected.

Parents, as well as teachers, often reinforce the behavior they think is undesirable. When Daddy comes home at the end of an exhausting day and collapses into his chair in front of the T.V., he gives no attention to the children playing nicely in the other room. When is his attention given? When a loud shriek assaults his tender nerve ends, that's when. Analysis: The appropriate playing is ignored, and the inappropriate gets attention. Exactly the reverse should occur.

Reinforce The Desirable; Ignore The Undesirable

If you are very consistent from the very beginning, most unwanted classroom behavior can be eliminated by systematically ignoring it while giving immediate praise and attention for its desirable opposite. If a book is dropped while you are talking to a student, you do not even hear it. You don't falter in mid-sentence, but continue on with unbroken fluency as though the event never occurred; and you praise those who are working well and have their books neatly in their desks (where they can't drop).

One child raises his hand, while another says, "Teacher, teacher." A teacher who understands the reinforcing power of her attention is stone-deaf in this situation. Immediate attention goes to the child with his hand up. Fine so far, but that is only half the procedure. The next step requires the teacher to watch very carefully for a raised hand from the child who started by saying "Teacher, teacher." It is only when the child is ignored for calling out *and* reinforced for hand raising that the desirable behavior is taught.

Don't underestimate it. This tactic of simultaneously ignoring one behavior and heavily reinforcing its opposite is very powerful. To be effective, however, it has to be applied with absolute consistency. If the no talking rule is in and a teacher accidentally responds with a "That's a good idea" to someone who talks out, she's in trouble. This puts her attention on an intermittent schedule which makes talking out much harder to reduce. Teacher attention is then like the jackpot on a slot machine. You don't get it every time, but if you stay with it long enough, you will. "Teacher, teacher, teacher, teacher, ..." Any time the ignore-one-reinforce-the-other strategy is used, the undesired behavior must be *always* ignored. Teacher attention is a very powerful reinforcer for most children. Just as with the "sit down" example, reprimands and scolding have often been found to act as reinforcers even though the teacher intended just the opposite.

The other requirement is that the teacher who uses this technique must *always be alert to catch the children being good.* Unfortunately there is a tendency to just enjoy the ride when things are going well and leap to action only when things start to go bad. The key to preventing problems is to remain constantly active in teaching and praising the behaviors that are desired.

Time Out From Positive Reinforcement

There are some behaviors which compete with effective learning that cannot be ignored. When one child stands up and hits another in the mouth, you can't pretend it didn't happen. If a child crawls out onto the fire escape, you don't ignore it.

Every classroom has rules. Good classrooms don't seem to have very many, but there are always clear prohibitions placed on behaviors that can injure people or damage property. These rules need to be stated clearly and without elaboration. Once that is done, the stage is set for insuring that the rules are followed. Any rule violation must meet with an *immediate* consequence which will deter a repetition and provide a clear example for other children.

"Time Out" is the label given to a procedure which carries the full title of "Time out from positive reinforcement." Technically, it involves following any rule violation with the immediate removal of all possibility of reinforcement. Consequently, Time Out can be useful *only* when a rule violation occurs in a setting that contains lots of reinforcers. The logic is simple. If reinforcement is not present, there is no way to remove the offender from it.

Here's how it works. Suppose Tommy and Alan are working at the same table and Alan takes Tommy's pencil. The offended Tommy grabs the pencil back and pushes Alan to the floor. The entire encounter is brief, no one is hurt, nothing is damaged, and the danger is only potential. (The greatest danger may be that Tommy's aggression was reinforced by the recovery of the pencil.) This classroom, however has a rule which prohibits hitting, and a rule which prohibits taking other people's things. Each boy broke a rule.

The teacher moves quickly to both children and says something in the natural lexicon of teachers like, "You know the rules. In this class we don't hit and we don't take other people's things." Without further comment, each boy is seated in a chair which is moved four or five feet away from the rest of the children. The teacher sets a kitchen timer for three minutes, says, "As soon as the bell rings, you may join the group again," and returns to work with the other children. When the timer rings and the boys rejoin the group, the teacher resumes her attention to them as though the incident had never occurred.

Notice that the entire sequence is carried out in a non-emotional, matter-of-fact way. A rule is broken and there is an immediate consequence. The teacher does not scold, admonish, lecture, or moralize to the boys. In fact, she's hardly involved at all. The rule infraction initiates the Time Out and the bell ends it. It does not involve the personal mediation of the teacher which would make her the source of punishment and jeopardize her reinforcing properties. The children are not shamed or ridiculed. It is quite unnecessary to include gratuitous sermons like, "Go sit in that chair and think about your sins," or, "Sit there until you are ready to come back and act like little gentlemen."

The Time Out procedure must be precise, exactly timed to immediately follow the rule violation, and completely dispassionate.

Classrooms that use Time Out usually have a rule not found in other rooms, which states that you "don't talk to children that are in Time Out." There is another chair and another timer for any child who would speak to, taunt, or tease a timed out child. This rule is usually only broken once!

THE CLASSROOM SCENE

Combined, the last two chapters have dealt with a single critical issue: the more behavior children engage in, the more they are likely to learn.

The use of effective prompts and well-timed reinforcers can increase, strengthen, and refine children's behavior, but the sharp edge of the learning situation is dulled by commands and restrictions that unnecessarily suppress reasonable classroom behavior. Granted, there are cases where specific behaviors need to be reduced or eliminated because they interfere with effective learning. It is understandable that violence, aggression, and property damage are unacceptable in a classroom, but the control of these behaviors need not suppress all behavior or jeopardize the reinforcing quality of the teacher's attention.

With this general understanding, a few reflections are in order on some familiar classroom situations. Somehow, most of the rules of conduct that have been established in schools appear to support the convenience of the teacher rather than the learning of the children. Why, for example, do so many classrooms put a premium on quiet? Why does the reasonable rule of not talking while the teacher is talking become the unreasonable rule of not talking at all? Why do children have to line up and walk, mute, from place to place in elementary school? Why do children have to ask permission to go to the bathroom?

Remembering the classrooms you have known either as a student or a teacher, is it possible they might have been more attractive:

1. if the teacher had greater tolerance for noise and activity and recognized them as the basis for teaching rather than feared them as signs of "poor control"?
2. if there were fewer "Thou shalt nots"?
3. if the teacher were more willing to accept tardiness or daydreaming as an indication that more reinforcers needed to be built into the learning activity, and
4. if inappropriate behavior were given less attention and appropriate behavior given more?

Even when the building principal *insists* on a quiet room, a closed door can protect a relaxed and active class that is more reinforcing for everyone and a more effective learning environment for the children.

REFERENCE

Madsen, C. H. Jr., W. C. Backer, D. R. Thomas, L. Koser, and E. Plager, "An analysis of the reinforcing function of 'sit down' commands," in R. K. Parker (ed.), *Readings in Educational Psychology*. Boston: Allyn & Bacon, 1968.

6

Teaching Motivation

*. . . Children, like grownups,
enjoy the sense of achievement
derived from mastering a difficulty,
but this requires a consistency of
effort of which few are capable
without some outside encouragement.*

Bertrand Russell

Unless some care is taken, motivation can become the kind of circular pseudo-explanation for behavior that was discussed in Chapter 1. If a student succeeds, we agree he was well motivated; if he fails, we contend he lacked proper motivation. Notice the ease with which almost total responsibility for success or failure is shifted to the child — remember the "Excuses Not To Teach?"

In any classroom you can observe some children who are well motivated. They work energetically toward the completion of their tasks, ask questions about what they are doing, take interest in the answers, and are obviously excited over their conclusions. They do indeed demonstrate a sense of achievement derived from mastering a task. This is the kind of behavior which reflects a history of positive reinforcement for inquiry and independent problem solving.

In most classrooms, you can also find the poorly motivated student, the child who shows little sign of interest and spends more time looking out the window than he does asking questions or working on his own. This is the kind of behavior which reflects a history of punishment or sparse reinforcement.

Since it is the teacher who manages, or fails to manage, the delivery of reinforcement, the conclusion must be that motivation is taught. How strongly a child is motivated toward a particular subject or activity depends in large part on how effectively it has been reinforced by the teacher. *

THE NEED FOR INCENTIVES

Learning almost any new skill requires extra effort at the beginning. Later, as skill increases, the new behavior generates its own reinforcers. Initially, however, the extra effort and practice required do not correspond to the meager reinforcement available.

A well-developed reading skill is maintained by the pleasure found in prose and poetry, and the usefulness of being able to interpret signs and directions. There is little improvement in the control of one's environment as a result of learning to respond correctly to the letters *a* and *n*. The cold and wet, the cramped feet and the awkward positions associated with beginning skiing are not as reinforcing as the controlled speed and feeling of freedom that come with greater skill. Even playing the piano for your own amusement suggests a substantial proficiency. Few are amused by playing scales, right hand alone.

The search for a flexible and manageable reinforcement system begins with recognizing the need for the temporary supplementary support of the early stages of learning a new task.

TEACHER SELECTED REINFORCERS

It has already been established that the approval and praise of the teacher is an effective reinforcer for most young children. When the teacher approves of a child's performance and exclaims, "That's *very* good!" the sequence is begun that can lead the child to better and better performances. The teacher who has learned to praise only those children who are working, while ignoring those who are off task, enjoys a setting where most of the children are on task most of the time. Praise for working faster can accelerate the children's progress, and excited approval for a novel idea can stimulate deviations from the norm that approach the bizarre. Praise can usually be counted on to strengthen the specific behavior that receives it, but praise is only one of several reinforcement strategies that a teacher has available.

Privileges are also granted as a consequence of good performance. When a teacher decides who will be first in the lunch line, or who will carry the ball out for recess, or who will take a message to the principal's office, and those decisions are explicitly linked to good classroom performance, a powerful reinforcement system is in operation. It is no accident that the contingent delivery of privileges is a favorite technique in all kinds of situations — it has limitations, but it works very well. The greatest dangers inherent in the delivery of contingent privileges are (a) they can lead to a competitive situation which produces more losers than winners, and (b) without explicit public criteria, the subjectivity of the teacher can lead to inequities.

NEGOTIATED REINFORCERS

In an expanded and elaborated form, the contingent delivery of privileges becomes a system of more or less formalized agreements, or contracts, between teacher and students. By prior agreement it might be decided that ten correct math problems earn five minutes of free time, twenty problems earn ten minutes, and so on. Contingency contracting is a system that makes excellent use of reinforcers to provide a solid incentive to otherwise difficult or tedious learning tasks. Although there are ways to avoid it, contingency contracting can generate unwanted and unproductive bargaining over the relative merit of a particular task or the value of a particular privilege.

A more sophisticated and less explicit form of contracting is seen in middle- and upper-grade classes that assign relatively large units of work in several areas and then expand or restrict privileges on the basis of the students' completion rates. For those who have been taught to use it wisely, the system is very attractive. On Monday the student receives his assignments for the week in Language Arts, Mathematics, Science, and Social Studies. Throughout the week he can set his own pace, decide when he is going to work on what for how long, and he can ask for help as needed. When not working, he has free access to the resource areas of the school. As long as his end-of-week checkouts are up to par, he remains free to manage his own time. Closer supervision only results when his performance drops. If all of this sounds too utopian, don't forget the catch phrase at the beginning of the description, "For those who have been *taught* to use it . . . ." Self-scheduling is the end-product of a very careful instructional sequence.

STUDENT SELECTED REINFORCERS: THE TOKEN ECONOMY

When activities the children prefer are available as a direct consequence of a particular behavior, the preferred activities become reinforcers which can generate and sustain motivation and progress. If these same activities are available automatically, regardless of what the child may do, they have little reinforcing value. The timing of the consequence and its clear relationship to a particular behavior make a crucial difference. Consequences that *immediately* follow a behavior can reinforce. If they are delivered too soon or too late, they will have little or no effect. Timing is the key.

The importance of delivering reinforcers immediately presents a problem. No classroom could operate with a system that sent a child out to play immediately after each correct answer or cooperative act. The solution is a token system. As each child in the class works at various learning tasks, he is given tokens for his progress and improvement. Every token presented provides encouraging approval without interrupting the child's work. Later in the day the accumulated tokens can be exchanged for events and activities that are important to each individual child. Over time, these backup activities give meaning and value to the tokens. As long as the backups are exciting and enjoyable, the tokens will support the child's motivation to learn and to succeed.

Because they can be delivered immediately, tokens provide needed support for the early steps in the development of a skill. As the skill improves to the point where continued progress is insured by the reinforcers the skill produces, the token support is withdrawn from that activity and shifted to another which is just getting started. Consequently, the way a child earns tokens is constantly changing. At first, tokens and praise will follow a child's first attempt at holding a pencil correctly. Later, with improved skill, tokens and praise follow the writing of a complete sentence.

Any number of activities and events could be used to support the early steps of learning a new skill, but the tokens have some clear advantages. A token can be delivered quickly (immediately after an improved behavior [a closer approximation]); it does not interrupt what the child is doing; and it can be exchanged later for any and all of the enjoyable things that may be available.

The token system is a powerful teaching tool which:

1. allows reinforcement to be delivered individually,

2. provides children with an unusual degree of self-determination as they exercise the right to choose how they will exchange their accumulated tokens,

3. maintains a balanced exchange system between teacher and children, a positive reciprocal social relationship rather than an authoritarian one,

4. establishes a noncompetitive learning situation where the dangers of being a loser are eliminated.

A great deal of scientific research has documented the benefits of token systems during the past few years, but for present purposes the important point is simply that children learn better when their progress is immediately reinforced.

A token can be any object, but during the early grades it is best if the token is an object which the child can hold and put in his pocket. It might be a match stick, a marble, a cardboard disc, a popsicle stick, or a plastic poker chip. At higher grade levels pencil marks on slips or check marks in special booklets can be used in the same way. Regardless of their physical form, the tokens function much like the trading stamps given out by merchants as an incentive for further shopping in their stores.

TOKEN DELIVERY

The complete exchange cycle in the token system involves three steps: behavior, token delivery, exchange. The nature of the behavior, the delivery procedure, and the nature of the exchange all vary according to the backgrounds of the children and the amount of experience they have had with token systems. In any form, however, it is necessary that the token acquire reinforcing properties of its own. Initially, a poker chip or check mark do not have any special value; they are not automatically or inherently reinforcing. They *become* reinforcers. How quickly the reinforcing properties of a token are established depends a great deal on how they are introduced.

Getting Things Started — Initial Exchanges

Young children in the preschool and primary grades quickly learn to value tokens as a result of their experience with them. Consequently, rather than holding a group meeting to discuss the rules of the new system, it is easiest to establish the procedures by putting them to use. A preschool teacher may want to teach her children to hang up their coats as soon as they enter the room. By moving immediately to the child who has just done so, the teacher can present a token as she says, "Thank you for hanging up your coat, Sally." Then, "Sally, if you wish, you may exchange your token to play with the doll house or a truck." The entire sequence of behavior, token, and exchange is accomplished in a few moments, and Sally has experienced her first learning episode in the use and value of tokens. The token was only mentioned once, but the message is clear. The rapid establishment of an effective token system requires frequent episodes where the entire exchange sequence quickly follows improved or desirable behavior.

Over the next several days, the items and activities for which the children may exchange tokens are varied and the time between the token delivery and an exchange opportunity is gradually increased. As different numbers of tokens are exchanged for events of different importance to the children, the reinforcing value of the token is quickly established. Regardless of the age or grade level of the children, tokens become reinforcers as a function of the value of the things for which they can be exchanged, and the frequency of exchange opportunities. Consequently, it is particularly important at the outset that tokens be delivered as often as possible.

Tokens Are Always Delivered With Praise

There has already been frequent reference to the reinforcing value of adult approval and praise. In fact, praise and approval *are* tokens. They are reinforcers which have been established through their association with other reinforcers. Praise and comments of commendation don't come just before a spanking or penalty; they nearly always precede favors and privileges. Combining the tokens with praise enhances both.

As the token and praise are simultaneously delivered, the event can be further embellished and personalized. "That's good writing, Timmy. Now do the next row just as well." "Thank you for listening so carefully, Sally." "I like the way you put your book away when you were through with it, Dan." All of these statements illustrate two desirable features of praise statements. First, the child's name is used. In addition to personalizing the contact between teacher and child, this practice takes advantage of the fact that the sound of one's own name is a positive event for most of us. Second, the praise very specifically identifies what behavior the teacher found commendable.

Token Delivery Is Individualized

Tokens are seldom delivered according to some standard that applies equally to all the children in a class. Each individual child earns tokens for personal improvement and progress. Consequently, a teacher must continually be aware of the current performance capability of every student. Two children of different proficiencies working side by side on the same subject will receive tokens and praise for different behaviors. For the skillful child, the token may follow the correct and rapid completion of an entire page of work. For the less skilled child, every other problem solution may be quickly followed by reinforcement. For a third child, the simple act of opening his book to the right page may be an occasion for wild celebration and great praise. Tokens are given to strengthen *any* behavior the teacher thinks important.

The tokens cannot work unless the children receive them and have the opportunity to exchange them. There is a tendency for teachers who are new to token systems to be too demanding. They want to reserve tokens for extra special performance and unusual merit. Such a posture interferes with the necessity for the frequent and immediate support of individual improvement. Shaping is a process that proceeds by approximations, not all at once.

IDENTIFYING POSSIBLE BACKUP ACTIVITIES

David Premack is an experimental psychologist who has worked primarily with laboratory animals, and has not been particularly interested in developing procedures for applied work. Nevertheless, one of the most useful tools in applied work carries the label, *Premack's Principle*. Roughly stated, Premack's Principle observes that, given any two behaviors of different strength, the stronger can be used to reinforce the weaker. For example, if you know a child who would rather sail boats in the sink than do math problems, sailing can be used as a reinforcer for math. The trick is to arrange the two properly. "As soon as you complete these twenty problems correctly, you may sail your boats for ten minutes."

The key to using Premack's Principle is the careful observation of children's preferences. In any situation where a child has access to a number of activities, the one he chooses can be correctly labeled a reinforcer. Any time a class is given free time, a number of probable reinforcers will be identified by the children's choices. Some children will select individual activities; others will demonstrate a preference for peer associations. Whatever they choose can be added to the list of backup reinforcers for that group. The token system then arranges to use Premack's Principle by making these things available to the children contingent on different numbers of tokens.

That's fine as far as it goes, but obviously children's preferences change, and they change often. The preferred activity of Monday may be low on the list by Wednesday; and often the nine o'clock preference is a drag by noon. This is particularly true when backups are largely things (toys, balls, trucks, puzzles, crayons, etc.) instead of activities (walks, treasure hunts, ongoing projects, and organized games). As children grow more experienced and skilled in handling a limited set of toys and "things," their familiarity coincides with diminishing excitement. At the same time, however, social situations become an almost constant challenge because they are never the same twice. Any situation composed of several people will contain unique aspects that can be very reinforcing.

At the very first exchange mentioned earlier, a single token could be exchanged for a favorite toy. That is a good opening because it gets the exchange sequence going quickly and quite dependably. Very quickly, however, the system becomes more sophisticated. The list of backups contains fewer and fewer objects, and more and more activities. At one point, ten minutes of recess may be a strong backup. Later, plain recess may be available at some minimal price (indicating lower preference), but there will be a higher premium attached to a recess activity organized and participated in by the teacher. Long-term group projects can be outstanding and very durable backups. Building an entire model city out of match sticks and toothpicks is an example. Initially, exchanging tokens for the necessary building materials is likely to be an individual matter. Later, as the project becomes more elaborate, every member of the building team will want to be present at every session. Eggshell mosaics and other elaborate art projects offer great possibilities. Long-term science projects with batteries, buzzers, and bulbs are great because each encounter with these materials can increase the child's preference for a return session. Writing a story, reading toward obtaining a certificate (suitable for framing) declaring that 10, 20, or 30 books have been read; having time and materials to illustrate a composition; having the opportunity to tutor (or be tutored by) a classmate are soon more effective motivators than a toy or a chance to color a picture. Yes, it does involve extra planning and effort. Yes, it works well enough to be more than worth it.

The progression through the various types of backups which has just been described is a fairly long process. Two or three years may be required to move from frequent short-term reinforcement to the more sophisticated long-term backups. Throughout, it is the careful observation of the children's preferences that allows for the construction of the most attractive list of backups which the children may select from in exchange for their accumulated tokens.

SETTING PRICES

Every exchange opportunity needs to be well planned in advance. Ad hoc exchanges generated on the spur of the moment are likely to produce spending opportunities that are not very exciting. A child who doesn't enjoy the products of his labors is apt to labor less in the future and the whole reinforcement program is jeopardized. Each exchange opportunity needs to be formulated in a list of at least six specific activities that will be available and the approximate prices that each will require (some of which include the teacher as a participant). The lists need to avoid a dull routine which re-presents the same half-dozen items over and over as regularly as beans come up on the lunch menu. At irregular intervals there need to be surprise events that are new and unfamiliar to the children. Remember a cool breeze on a hot day and you can recognize that the quality of a good thing is enchanced when it comes unexpectedly.

Preferences Determine Prices

When a list of backups is prepared for each exchange period, set the price that each activity will require. Each price should reflect the preference the children have shown toward the event, and every list needs to contain activities of different prices. The range of prices may be adjusted according to the amount and type of earning period that immediately precedes the exchange, but that adjustment should be made when the list is prepared. Some lessons facilitate higher rates of earning, so it's reasonable that the price of commodities needs to vary to stay in line with purchashing power. It is the variations in earning opportunity that need to influence backup prices, however, and not momentary variations in teacher disposition. That's the safeguard of advance planning.

When prices are set at the end of an earning period rather than at the beginning, problems can arise. A tenderhearted teacher who lowers the price of a backup for the attractive and cooperative child who has not earned because he has not been working is throwing away contingent reinforcement. Reinforcement needs to be strictly contingent on appropriate behavior, for if it follows inappropriate behavior, that is what it will strengthen. Another danger in after-the-fact price setting is generated when the teacher who just can't seem to get around to attend to the children at her usual rate lowers prices correspondingly. Both of these adjustments corrupt the exchange system. By setting the prices according to the children's preferences and the opportunity to earn — and doing so before the fact — the appropriate contingencies are maintained for everyone, teachers and children. Children who goof off risk missing out on their most preferred activity, and teachers who goof off have to face the disappointment of the children. However harsh it may sound, both of these consequences help to correct problems before they become debilitating habits.

Prices on given backups will also vary from time to time according to the shifting preferences the children display. Teachers soon learn how to use good sales appeal, premiums, discount sales, and attractive packaging to maintain a high level of motivation. Obviously it works. These are the same techniques which merchants and advertisers use to provide consistent incentive for our earning and spending behaviors. Where there is a real doubt about the relative attractiveness of two items, set the prices on them the same and count the number of children who choose each. The one with the most takers gets a higher price tag next time.

THE TRANSACTION

Even though prices are established when the lists of backups are drawn up, they are not announced to the children in advance. Advance notice of prices can lead the children to earn only until they have accumulated enough for their preference and then just cool it for the rest of the period.

When an earning period ends, the teacher only needs to say, "Thank you for putting your book away, Martin. I'll put up the list of activities and their prices so you can decide if you would like to exchange for something." (As in other situations, the invitation to Martin is just as effective as shouting to the whole class. The word gets around.) Martin makes his choice, counts out the necessary number of tokens, and moves out to begin his selected activity. The teacher moves on to repeat similar transactions with other children.

Tickets

Tickets (small slips of paper) can be very handy for some backups. If the basic price for recess, for example, is 10, but an organized game during recess is 15, a ticket can make transactions smoother. Children who only want (or can only afford) plain recess pay their 10 tokens and are ready to go. Those who elect the game pay 15 and receive a ticket. A few moments later, on the playground, the teacher collects the tickets and the game begins without having to debate whether Sally paid 10 or 15.

VARIABILITY IN EXCHANGES

One way to take advantage of the superior properties of *variable* reinforcement schedules is to throw in surprise goodies on top of regular events. Suppose, for example, 23 of the children in a class have exchanged for a variety of backups. Four children are sitting the period out. One child was off task most of the previous earning period so he didn't have enough for this exchange, and the other three are saving the tokens for some unknown future activity. This is a fine time to add a bonus item to the period without any extra charge. It may be a five-minute extension on the period, a sudden trip to the auditorium to see a film (obviously surprises are also planned in advance), or some other surefire goodie. The point is that the extra activity is only available to those who have already exchanged to participate in the backup period. The tactic does two things. First, it enhances the backup for those who contact the bonus; and second, it serves as an added incentive for the four who opted out of this period. There is no need to call attention to the obvious fact that the nonparticipants are missing out. Without further prompting, the chances are that the four reluctant traders will be first in line when the next exchange opportunity arrives.

As teachers begin to get exciting and powerful backup periods arranged, another refinement can be added. Just as it is important to include surprise events to exchange periods, it is also effective to announce exchanges at surprise times. If backup periods usually follow 40-minute instruction periods, announce a sudden exchange after only 20 minutes. The prices will be scaled down, of course, but there will still be the entire list of events and a range of prices. With some practice, instructional periods of 20, 38, 24, 43, 35, 25, 50, and 32 minutes can mix things up to produce an even more effective incentive system.

It probably should not be stressed, but the principle in varying the length of the earning periods is the same one that hooks people on slot machines or bingo games. Since you never know in advance when a jackpot is going to turn up, the only way to beat the game is to stay with it every minute. It doesn't have anything to do with whether or not the children can tell time. If reinforcement is available after fixed time intervals over a long period, even laboratory animals can discriminate well enough that they learn to work slowly at the beginning of the interval and with greater enthusiasm only as the time for reinforcement draws near.

ENDING THE EXCHANGE PERIOD

The transition out of an exchange should be as smooth and rapid as the transition into it. The most dependable procedure is the easiest. At the end of the exchange period, the teacher simply announces in a quiet, matter-of-fact way, "Trading time is over now." As the first child leaves his backup activity and joins the teacher, the lesson begins *immediately*. The first child to arrive gets the instant attention of the teacher and lots of praise and tokens as he gets going on his assignment. Rather than nagging the children who are slow with, "Hurry up," or "We're waiting, William," any who wish to do so may purchase a five-minute extension on the backup period. If a five-minute extension is available for the original price of the event, few will take the option. It's tough to make lessons compete effectively with strong backups, but it can be done. A set of conditions needs to be established that creates a reinforcement differential favoring a prompt return to instructional activity.

PROBLEMS TO BE AVOIDED

The implementation of a token exchange system may sound like a cumbersome, time-consuming practice that could not possibly yield benefits commensurate with the effort needed to maintain it. True, it does take careful planning and some practice, but an increasing number of teachers at all grade levels are sufficiently reinforced by the dramatic effects of the system that its adoptions are increasing rapidly. Perhaps the biggest return for the effort comes from the virtual elimination of management problems which lead to hassles, commands, threats, and punishment. When strong positive reinforcement is differentially applied to appropriate and desirable behavior, misconduct and low motivation are seldom observed. Teaching well behaved, highly motivated children is the challenge that all teachers are ready to accept. Any novel or unconventional procedure becomes familiar and comfortable only with practice. To make the early practice period more reinforcing for the teacher, a few cautions need to be observed.

*Tokens Are Never Mentioned By The Teacher Except
To Announce Prices*

In the first flush of excitement that accompanies initial observations of the dramatic impact of effective exchanges it can be difficult for teachers to avoid bargaining with the children. Nevertheless, any mention of tokens except to announce prices, quickly leads to undesirable patterns. Unnecessary comments can compromise the entire system in a number of ways. For example:

> Bribing: "If you'll do the next three problems, I'll give you another token."
> Hawking: "Who would like to help me for three tokens?"
> Threatening: "If you don't get busy, you won't have enough tokens for recess."

In all of these cases and many others, the statements of the teacher lead to counter statements by the children and then to bargaining. For example: "How many tokens is this worth?" "I'll do it for four tokens." "Can I have a token?" If such statements are given any attention at all the classroom quickly fills with small-scale labor-management struggles with each side trying to maximize its profits (reinforcers). Since the tokens are intended to support and sustain ongoing activity, they must be given in a way that does not consummate a contract and terminate the behavior they are supposed to strengthen. Tokens are given as a *result* of a desirable approximation and never used to coax or bribe a behavior. The teacher who gives attention to the children's attempts to bargain quickly loses control of the system. Problems are ahead whenever children are reinforced for successful bargaining and talking about tokens instead of for progress on their assignments.

Charity Is Not Always A Virtue

Teachers new to token systems are occasionally tempted to extend credit or charity to children who fail to earn enough for a particular activity. Either practice, of course, destroys the effective contingency and quickly drives the teacher into a corner. If a child's preferred activity is priced at 10 tokens and he only has 9, he simply misses that backup and selects a less preferred one within his means. It is quite inappropriate for the teacher to comment about the situation. The whole transaction needs to be handled in a matter-of-fact way with no recriminations, admonishments, or moral injunctions. The child who misses his first preference at one exchange is most likely to work his head off during the next instruction period to be first in line with a surplus of tokens at the next exchange opportunity.

If, however, a child repeatedly lacks enough tokens for his high preference backups, some immediate checking is in order. The problem may be with the teaching. One possibility is that the child is being presented with instructional tasks that are too difficult for his present skills. In this case, no matter how hard he tried, he may not be skillful enough to earn at an appropriate rate. Another possibility is that, even though he has been working diligently and effectively, the teacher has not been monitoring his progress closely enough. Both of these situations can lead to a reduction in the value of the token as a reinforcer. After all they can't be very valuable if they can't be exchanged for other things of value.

These two problems (the child who is misplaced in materials and the child who is ignored) are highlighted by the token system. (The visability of the child without tokens provides excellent insurance that such problems will be quickly solved.) Adjusting prices in a spirit of charity can allow either of these problems to continue uncorrected.

Fairness Is In The Earning, Not The Spending

Observers in token classrooms have occasionally expressed concern over the *fairness* of setting the same price on a recess game for all children. "Doesn't that give an advantage to the more skillful child — the one who can earn more?" If every child was awarded a token for each page completed, it certainly would be unfair since some would be able to complete two or three pages a day and others might only complete one. That's not the way token reinforcement works. It is worth repeating that the tokens are given for progress and improvement in each individual child's performance. Effective teachers concentrate on shaping behavior rather than paying for set products. One child may earn five tokens for ten pages of work while the child next to him earns his five tokens for ten problems. Consequently, the specific contingencies of reinforcement will vary according to each child's current performance level, but the cost of participation is standardized. Every child has an equal opportunity to earn.

The rule of equal opportunity to earn means that children may earn different amounts of tokens for the same amount of work. Realizing this, the skeptical observer may ask how to deal with the situation where one child complains, "She got a token for that, why didn't I?" Since it has already been established that tokens are never mentioned, this is a good illustration of a situation where it is proper to ignore the question. If you stop to explain the rationale behind the different schedules of reinforcement, you are reinforcing the questioning and can expect it to increase. If a teacher never mentions tokens except to announce prices, the children will follow the same pattern. If statements and questions about tokens *never* get a reaction from the teacher, they simply will not occur.

A Slow System Is A Loser

The success of a token system, particularly in the early stages, is a direct function of the speed with which the tokens are dispensed and exchanged. A token delivered at 9:00 A.M. is not going to be a very big deal if there is no opportunity to exchange it until 2:45 that afternoon. Because the reinforcing value of the token is determined by what it can be exchanged for, more frequent exchange opportunities will correspond to higher levels of motivation.

Similarly, low rates of dispensing tokens are not consistent with the principles of shaping. It has been observed before that the more often improvements can be reinforced, the more quickly behaviors will change. More reinforcement leads to more behavior, more behavior leads to more reinforcement, etc. In an effective token classroom it is not uncommon to see a teacher dispense tokens at the rate of 120 to 125 per hour.

Summary

A token system is a way of emphasizing the improvements in children's behavior, and it provides tangible evidence of a teacher's approval. It sets up a system where children do not have to be coaxed and urged to "Get busy!" "Hurry up!" and "Pay attention!" The children work actively at their various tasks because of the positive consequences which result. It creates a classroom where children have the chance to participate on their own terms instead of just taking orders. Most of us prefer that kind of arrangement, and children are certainly no different.

Tokens are always associated with positive events. When they are received they are accompanied with praise and encouragement, and when they are spent it is in exchange for things the children value. Tokens are never associated with unpleasant events. They are never taken away from a child for misbehavior (unless he puts one in his mouth which creates a physical danger); there are no fines, no taxes, and no dues in a token system. Neither are they associated with any kind of pressure or coercion. It is completely inconsistent to say, "Hurry up or you won't earn enough tokens for recess games." However gentle the statement may be, it is still a threat, and tokens must never be associated with threats.

A token system is designed to provide immediate tangible positive reinforcement for improved behavior. If the system provides a wide range of exciting backup events, has variable prices, occasional bonuses, and unpredictable exchange opportunities, it will guarantee a consistently high level of motivation for all of the children.

If all of this seems like crass commercialism quite unbefitting the hallowed precincts of a school, think about the alternatives. To return to an earlier point, the alternative to coercion and threat is not boundless permissiveness or anarchy. The real alternative to coercion is the presentation of choices and options. Teachers are in the business of designing robust, exciting, challenging classrooms where learning is constantly associated with fun things. The magic word is "choice." Children, free to choose, learn very quickly that every choice has a consequence, and some choices are more rewarding than others. When a teacher learns how to create attractive alternatives, the problem of motivation and the need for coercion evaporates.

7

Getting It All Together

When our sciences of human nature and human relations are anything like as developed as are our sciences of physical nature, their chief concern will be with the problem of how human nature is most effectively modified. The question will not be whether it is capable of change, but of how it is to be changed under given conditions. This problem is ultimately that of education in its widest sense.

John Dewey, 1938

The behavioral principles previously described are all extensions of and elaborations on the fundamental principle which states: *behavior is a function of its consequences.*

Generalizations do occur; discriminations develop; shaping progresses; and elaborate behavioral chains are created whether or not we deliberately do anything about it. Like the laws of physics or genetics, the basic laws of behavior are not changed by our knowledge or ignorance of them. Anyone may choose to ignore the existence of these principles, but they will continue to operate. Behavior will continue to be shaped by the consequences it encounters.

The natural social and physical environment of every child provides all kinds of consequences. That's the problem. Because there are *all kinds*, some consequences will shape desirable social behaviors and some will be equally effective in shaping undesirable behaviors. Further, while natural consequences will shape *some* desirable behaviors, they cannot be relied on to develop *all* the complex skills needed to manage our contemporary social environment. Some children will encounter natural contingencies in their environment that will shape reading skill; most children will not. Some children will develop more than adequate skill in public school classrooms as they exist today; many children will not.

With a practical knowledge of the principles of behavior, however, a whole new range of opportunities is opened to teachers and parents. We need no longer wait and hope for the happy environmental accident that creates a skillful child. With a working knowledge of behavioral contingencies, teachers can design instructional environments that will quickly alter children's behaviors in predictable ways. They can design environments that will teach.

LEARNING IS A PERSONAL PROCESS

An obvious, if unstated, theme of this book has been that behavior analysis applies to one student at a time. The known principles of behavior provide for the development of interaction patterns between teacher and student that can have very predictable outcomes. Even in those cases where the careful analyses of behavior are more work than traditional teaching strategies, the improved outcomes are appropriate compensation. A teacher who has learned how to provide reinforcing consequences for improvements in a child's behavior enjoys a special kind of relationship with that child.

Every teaching sequence begins by determining what each child needs to be taught. This objective is then translated into a set of observable behaviors that define the terminal performance. That's the target — some collection of behaviors which lets the student show that he has learned what the teacher set out to teach.

With that target in mind, the teacher then tries to select the appropriate beginning for the shaping process with each individual child. Shaping has already been defined as the differential reinforcement of successive approximations of the final performance. That jargon-laden phrase was then translated to emphasize the importance of immediately reinforcing each new improvement in a child's behavior. Although both are accurate statements and it is quite true that the shaping process will systematically alter the form and strength of behavior, it is also true that shaping is a delicate, almost artistic, procedure.

SUCCESSFUL SHAPING

A successful shaping sequence depends on a number of factors. The first, a clearly defined final performance, is required as a constant reference so an approximation can be recognized. You can only know if you're getting closer if you know the ultimate goal. Similarly, the entry inventory establishes the starting point so it is possible to recognize an improved approximation. With the starting and end points established, it's now possible to get on with the important business of prompting lots of behavior so that reinforcement can be differentially applied to each improvement in the behavior. Now we get to the tricky question of, "How big an improvement should occur before reinforcement is delivered?"

There is no pat answer to the question, but there are some guides that allow a teacher to recognize if the reinforcement is being delivered too often or not often enough. Being able to recognize and correct for problems is probably the closest we can get to a statement of how to shape.

It will help to recall the strategy, described in the second chapter, which Charlie's teacher used to shape up (increase) his time on task to the point she thought necessary for beginning reading instruction. By observing and keeping records she determined that Charlie was frequently on task for five minute intervals so she began the process by carefully attending to him after he had been engaged in an activity for that period of time. Next, she increased the requirement to six minutes on task, and simultaneously avoided giving him any attention for shorter periods. As she continued restricting her attention to longer intervals, Charlie's on task periods gradually changed their distribution so that more of them were longer (as long as 12 minutes) and fewer of them were less than four minutes.

Ratio Strain

Now, suppose that the teacher had abruptly decided to withhold all of her attention until Charlie spent a continuous period of 15 minutes on task. Since a 15-minute interval did not exist in the record of Charlie's on task periods, the teacher might have to ignore him completely. If the reinforcement criterion is higher than the child's current range of behaviors, reinforcement will stop — extinction will start. With no reinforcement coming from the teacher for his on task behaviors, Charlie, quite predictably, would seek out other more reinforcing activities: throwing blocks, hitting Sigmund, melting crayons on the radiator, etc. None are particularly desirable, yet each is very likely to be quickly followed by the reinforcing attention of the teacher. The process just described — setting a requirement beyond the student's current range of behaviors and causing extinction to begin and shaping to stop — is called ratio strain. Ratio strain refers to the breakdown in behavior that results from a sudden increase in the ratio between the performance required and the reinforcement delivered. A student who has not mastered the division process is placed in algebra. Unable to solve the problems presented, none of his algebra behaviors are reinforced. In this setting no reinforcement is available; extinction results, and the child's progress stops.

A high school student is required to prepare a report based on his outlines of three reference books. Since he has never been taught to outline, his chances for reinforcement are nil, and the consequences of extinction are evidenced by disinterest, truancy, and misconduct. These examples may seem harsh, but the consequences of ratio strain are as serious as they are prevalent. They are prevalent because we persist in moving children to more advanced settings on the basis of their age rather than on the basis of their individual skills.

Remembering that ratio strain is caused by holding reinforcement contingent on performances which are currently beyond the student's capability should immediately suggest that appropriate remedy. Reduce the requirement for reinforcement. Select an approximation that is within the available range of behaviors, a smaller approximation of the final goal. Don't require Charlie to stay on task for 15 unbroken minutes when his longest interval to date has been 12. In seeking closer and closer approximations to the final performance, be sure each step is established in some strength before moving on to the next. If the rate of the behavior begins to decline, simply drop back to an earlier step and build it up again. The error of moving to an advanced approximation which results in ratio strain too quickly can then be avoided.

Stereotyping

Another error that can stop the shaping process is called stereotyping. In this case the continued reinforcement of a common form of a behavior gradually reduces the range of behavior variations available for further shaping. The teacher who repeatedly praised Charlie after exactly five minutes of task behavior could quickly establish a pattern whereby he would stop at the end of every five-minute study interval to wait for teacher approval. Other familiar examples of this breakdown in the shaping process are provided by the child who waits for teacher attention at the end of each page of reading, each problem in a math book, or each helpful act in the classroom. It misses the point to suggest that children who display these kinds of behavior are "attention seeking" or "overly dependent." Like other undesirable behaviors that have been discussed, these patterns exist because *they have been taught*. It was not intended, but without appropriate contingency management, these behaviors were developed by the reinforcement contingencies operating in the classroom. Stereotyped behavior like that described can be not only annoying to the teacher who has to contend with great quantities of "See what I did" demands, but more importantly, it is a signal that progress (shaping) is threatened. Reductions in the range of variations in a student's behavior make it more difficult to find and reinforce the closer approximations necessary to continue shaping.

The solution is: Be brave! There is still some variability left in the behavior. Even though better approximations may be slight, they do exist. Waiting until they occur and then providing strong differential reinforcement will unlock the behavior and get the shaping process going once again.

Variability Strengthens The Theme

The cause of the stereotyping problem, together with the recommendation for its correction, may serve to recall the observations in the preceding chapter about the advantages of building variability into reinforcement delivery. Varying the length of earning periods and the times and kinds of reinforcement should not suggest chaos or disorganization. Planned variation keeps things exciting! Pat, predictable schedules can lead to boredom and reduced productivity.

Suppose a teacher working with a small group on a math lesson contacts first one child and then another in a set pattern. The children will quickly develop some very predictable study behaviors. The attention each child gives to his lesson while the teacher is working with him is likely to cease when she moves to the next child in the sequence. Then, as she moves around the group in fixed order, he will gradually resume the lesson as she draws nearer so that he is again earnestly studying when next contacted. A child in a group of seven will often spend about two sevenths of his time actually engaged in the lesson material. A better method is the adoption of an unpredictable pattern of contacting children who are working in a small group. By moving from one on task child to another in a sequence that moves one way, then the other, then crisscrosses the group, a teacher can develop and sustain almost continuous on task behavior among all the children in the group. When reinforcement is delivered *only* when the children are on task and it is delivered with unpredictable variability, all the children's study behavior will be strong and persistent.

Notice that this procedure is almost the exact opposite of the distraction technique which is widely recommended in many methods classes. The distraction technique, you will remember, suggests you should immediately call on the unattending child. Presumably it is intended to be a mild aversive consequence for the discourtesy of inattention. A teacher who understands the principles of behavior can immediately recognize the dangers of such a procedure; the teacher's attention, which may be a strong reinforcer, is inappropriate for off task behavior and will not reinforce the appropriate on task behavior of the other children.

WHEN DO YOU STOP REINFORCEMENT?

This is a frequently asked question which deserves special attention. The question may arise because of a fallacious belief that reinforcement procedures are something new to classroom instruction. By this time it should be clear that there is nothing new about classroom reinforcement except our improved understanding of its role in the learning process.

Behavior is, and always has been, shaped by the reinforcing and punishing consequences attached to it. Consequently, one answer to the question is that there is no way to avoid reinforcing or punishing or the effects either will have.

Changing The Source Of Reinforcement

Another form of the question about removing reinforcement procedures stresses that it is the source and not the function of the reinforcement that is at issue. The procedure of planning the systematic delivery of teacher attention or tokens for specific behaviors is the novel element in the system. Questions from this orientation are generally phrased in terms of the relative advantages of "intrinsic" as opposed to "extrinsic" reinforcement. The issue may be overdrawn and enjoying more attention that it merits. First, there can be little, if any, disagreement over the obvious advantages of intrinsic reinforcement. Any activity which provides its own reinforcers whether in the form of self-satisfaction or the exercise of curiosity does not need extrinsic support. It may even eliminate the need for a teacher. It only remains then to consider what is appropriate in those cases where the activity does not provide its own reinforcers. One strategy is, "Don't worry. He'll mature." Although that could be acceptable in some areas, it can also be an excuse not to teach. The practicing teacher must still accept the responsibility of teaching young children to read. In other words, the day-to-day problem which the teacher must face is how to develop needed skills when the learning activity is not automatically reinforcing. The solution is provided by recalling some of the preceding chapter.

Learning almost any new skill requires extra effort at the beginning. Later, as skill increases, the new behavior generates its own reinforcers. In other words, a history of extrinsic reinforcement for a particular activity can develop skills so that the activity can become intrinsically reinforcing.

Secondary Reinforcers

At the beginning of a child's life there are only a few events which are automatically, or intrinsically, reinforcing. Food, air, and water are certainly on the list, but each addition requires more and more speculation. By the time a child enters school, there is a greatly expanded list of reinforcers which includes events such as smiles and praise of his mother and other adults, the companionship of peers, and a variety of toys, games, and social activities. Why so long a list? Because events associated with reinforcement become reinforcing themselves. Technically, to transform a neutral stimulus into a secondary reinforcer it is necessary that the neutral stimulus become discriminative (a direct antecedent) for reinforcement. An example is in order.

> A mother ministering to her newborn child is frequently in the position of delivering strong primary reinforcers by feeding, changing, and fondling the infant. Food is a primary positive reinforcer because it alleviates a state of physiological deprivation. The reinforcing food, however, is not delivered in isolation; the occasion is a social one and in all probability the mother is smiling and talking to the child as it is fed. The smile and the mother's voice in no way reduce the child's hunger, but they are present when the reinforcing event of feeding occurs. Indeed, when food is delivered, the smile and voice are, almost invariably, associated with it until they and even the sight of the mother's face take on reinforcing capabilities. The smile, originally neutral, has become a secondary reinforcer. (Adapted from Burgess and Bushell, 1969, p. 36.)

Most simply put, events and activities which repeatedly lead to reinforcement become reinforcing in and of themselves. It does not happen immediately, but over time one reinforcer can create another.

Initially there is nothing automatically, or intrinsically, reinforcing about a book. Nevertheless, if every time a child touched a book, reinforcement immediately followed, books would become very reinforcing. Initially, there may be little intrinsic reinforcement in a reading lesson, but if reading lessons were constantly associated with lavish reinforcement (even lavish extrinsic reinforcement), the very act of reading would become intrinsically reinforcing.

A technique which behavior analysis teachers frequently use to judge whether they are providing enough reinforcement in instructional (earning) periods combines this principle of secondary reinforcement with the Premack Principle. It will be recalled that the Premack Principle was used to identify children's reinforcers. Put a child in a situation where he can choose among several events and activities, and watch what he elects. The activity which he prefers can be used as a reinforcer. Following this procedure, teachers include reading and mathematics texts in the list of backups that also contains games and other special activities. When a child freely elects a reading text as a backup, the teacher can take satisfaction in the reinforcement level of her reading lessons. Reading has become a secondary (intrinsic) reinforcer.

When do you stop administering planned reinforcement? Even if you do not stop it entirely, the need for supportive reinforcement is reduced to the extent that:

1. the skill developed by supportive reinforcement brings the child into contact with natural reinforcers (e.g., playing a piano skillfully);
2. a strong history of supportive reinforcement has transformed a neutral activity into a secondary reinforcer.

Raising The Criterion For Reinforcement

As secondary, or natural, reinforcers progressively support more and more behavior there is less need for extrinsic reinforcement. Consequently, the entire process of education is devoted to the gradual development of behaviors which are independent of continuous teacher-delivered reinforcers. It may be called strong motivation or self-reliance, but it is easier to design procedures to teach reinforcement when you realize that it results from systematic increases in the amount of behavior required for each reinforcer.

By now it comes as no surprise to learn increases in the criterion for reinforcement can be designed by either increasing the amount of time between reinforcers or by increasing the number of instances of a behavior required for reinforcement. In the classroom there is usually a combination of both elements. In the early stages of a learning sequence, a small number of correct responses during a relatively long time interval will result in reinforcement. Later, as skills improve and a history of reinforcement has improved motivation, more correct behaviors will be required during a relatively shorter period of time.

DESIGNING EFFECTIVE CLASSROOMS

It is now possible to begin to use the principles of learning to sketch some of the more obvious requirements of effective classrooms. At the beginning of the long and complex learning sequence that makes up the elementary school there are some distinctive requirements. Initially, a high rate of student behavior is going to require very frequent reinforcement; and that reinforcement needs to be carefully managed so that it is always the immediate consequence of better approximations — improved behavior.

Can a single teacher effectively monitor and differentially reinforce the improving behaviors of thirty individual five-year-olds at one time? Not effectively. So we have contented ourselves with less ambitious terminal behaviors for kindergarten. Given the prevailing staffing pattern in kindergarten, the teacher has to be satisfied with monitoring and reinforcing a very small proportion of the total number of the children's behaviors. It is better than nothing, but a long way from meeting the requirements of an effective teaching situation.

Can a teacher effectively monitor and differentially reinforce the improving behaviors of thirty individual high school honor students? Quite effectively. This does not mean that the learning process is any different for these two groups. It does point out that the honor student has progressed to the point where large amounts of independent work can be sustained by relatively infrequent teacher-managed reinforcement. It is a situation brought about by a long history of shaping which has developed both a high level of skill and a number of secondary reinforcers. In spite of the obvious differences in the reinforcement requirements of these two groups, there is a surprising similarity in the teacher-student ratio in both kindergarten and high school.

If we base our design on the principles of behavior, kindergarten and prekindergarten children would be taught in environments that provide for the delivery of consequences to the greatest possible proportion of all their behaviors. A staff composed of one teacher for each six or seven children needs to be considered essential. "Teacher" is set off in quotes to recall from the opening chapter that anyone who provides reinforcement for a child's improvements is the one who changes the child's behavior — the one who teaches. That understanding allows us to look beyond the ranks of certified personnel for "teachers." Paraprofessionals, older more skillful children, and especially parents can all contribute to the design of better classrooms.

In the new classroom, the professional teacher manages a classroom team so it can provide the nearly continuous differential reinforcement that each individual child deserves. While the lead teacher is conducting a beginning reading lesson with a small group of six children, a similar group is working on a math lesson directed by a parent aide, another parent aide is teaching a group beginning handwriting skills, and a fifth grade boy is tutoring one child on some basic counting skills. It is all happening at one time, and every kindergarten child is experiencing the level of reinforcement needed to help him learn at his own maximum rate.

Children who get this kind of start in the elementary school sequence quickly acquire the motivation and skill that can support progressively more independent accomplishment. With intensive personalized instruction during the first two or three years, a foundation is built which can support continued individual progress even though the teacher-student ratio is decreased. For the third and fourth grades a classroom team can be built of the lead teacher, a full-time aide, and a half-time helper; and grades five and six can sustain effective individualized programs with a lead teacher and an aide.

Yes, these are high standards of quality, but it does not follow that they are impractical because of cost. If all of the cost factors of our present school systems are considered, it does not even follow that the staffing pattern would cost more than we are now paying. An examination of some current practices can illustrate the point.

Consider the familiar neighborhood kindergarten through sixth grade elementary school in a marginal to low-income area of town. There is a good chance it is named Jefferson and the building is well past voting age. The two kindergarten teachers each have a room to themselves where they meet one group of children each morning and another group each afternoon. Each grade level, first through sixth, has four classes with an average enrollment of 28.5 children. The school's total student enrollment of 790 children tumble into the arena every morning at the 8:40 bell and burst out again at 3:20 in the afternoon.

The kindergarten teachers in Jefferson do the best they can to fill each half-day session with the kinds of activities that will familiarize their children with school routines and customs. Through games, songs, and stories they find ingenious ways to improve the children's skills with basic number facts, letter symbols, relational concepts, and the names of objects, colors, and shapes. Most of all they try to make this initial school experience a pleasant one for the children as they learn to operate within an age-restricted peer group unlike any they have ever known before.

During the next year, the first grade teachers all concentrate on getting the children adjusted to a necessarily more regimented and task-oriented classroom scene. With careful attention to deportment, it is possible to arrange for short reading lessons with small groups of children as the remainder of the class is occupied with the ubiquitous ditto worksheets and workbooks. These procedures are adequate to get some of the children actually learning to read, but many just don't seem to be properly motivated and their progress is slow. By the end of that year a number of children have failed to reach the hoped for level of skill and if they move into the second grade it's with notes in their folders indicating a variety of probable and possible learning problems.

Within the next few years, an array of auxiliary and supportive personnel are assigned to remediate the accelerating difficulties of a growing number of children. A specialist reading teacher is on the scene relatively early to provide supplemental and remedial instruction. Some of the problems she encounters prompt a call to the district office requesting that the speech therapist spend two days, rather than just one, a week at Jefferson. The school psychologist is some help, but after all he has to split his time between Jefferson and Hay School, and Hay is really having much more serious problems. As the problems continue to mount, it is decided that it would be best to use a larger proportion of the school's Title I funds for additional units of the social worker's time. So many of the children's problems seem to be reflecting serious difficulties at home. In spite of the many extra services some of the children are receiving, there is little sign of improvement. Under these circumstances it is probably not surprising that a number of children are referred to the district's Special Education facility because their emotional and learning problems just cannot be properly handled at Jefferson.

I am afraid the elements of this sequence are as familiar as they are tragic and absurd. Thousands and thousands of dollars are being spent to remediate problems that should not have been created. To compound the tragedy, the specialists who work with a few children are substantially more expensive than a moderately salaried teacher. By failing to provide for the needs of individual children during the primary grades in a manner consistent with established principles of learning, we are faced with the enormous cost of attempting to remediate the resulting problems at a later date. The procedure is not remediating the problems of the children, it is attempting to remediate the problems of a system that must reexamine its own priorities. It would cost no more to do it right the first time around. Indeed, given the proliferation of specialists and social agencies that must be created to compensate for the consequences of ineffective education, the total costs to the community would probably be less.

COMMENCEMENT

Those in education, whether student or faculty, have a special appreciation for both of the meanings conveyed by the word commencement. As a ceremony, it marks the close of an academic season while simultaneously declaring the beginning of new careers. Both meanings are appropriate in the present context.

The preceding pages and chapters have, at best, been little more than an introduction to the scientific applications of behavior analysis in education. The brief scenario describing how a knowledge of the principles of behavior might influence the staffing of elementary classrooms is only a single example among countless possibilities. As young as it is, the field of behavior analysis has already given notice that an improved understanding of the learning process is leading to a coherent set of more effective teaching methods.

The techniques of behavior analysis will find application in more and more classrooms to the extent that two conditions are met. First, the behavior analysis programs now being implemented in classrooms throughout the country must demonstrate that they are effectively solving classroom problems which have not yielded to other approaches. There can be no question that the indications to date are extremely encouraging. The second necessary condition, of course, is that inservice as well as preservice teachers have the opportunity to learn to employ the methods and procedures of behavior analysis teaching.

The reader who has traveled the entire route to this point from the opening declaration, "Teachers change students' behaviors," is now ready to deal with the more sophisticated techniques and the supporting research of behavior analysis. In sum, the work represented by the bibliography which follows stands for the buoyant confidence and optimism shared by a growing number of research scientists and professional teachers. The classroom products of careful behavior analysis are tearing down the barriers which have prevented teachers from assuming full responsibility for the progress and achievement of their students. As each new technique is put into use, the improved performance of the children is more than adequate to reinforce the teacher's further contributions to behavior analysis teaching. No other process can offer greater encouragement.

REFERENCE

Burgess, Robert L. and Don Bushell, Jr., *Behavioral Sociology: The Experimental Analysis of Social Process.* New York: Columbia University Press, 1969.

Bibliography

PREPARED BY DON DORSEY

Becker, Wesley C., *Parents Are Teachers: A Child Management Program.* Champaign, Ill.: Research Press Company, 1971. 144 pp. Bibliography.

A clear and interestingly written self-study course developed especially for parents. Provides many practical suggestions for the uses of reinforcement techniques with children in everyday situations.

Order from: Research Press Company
2612 North Mattis Avenue
Champaign, Illinois 61820
($3.75, discounts on large orders)

Becker, Wesley C., Engelmann, Siegfried, and Thomas, Don R., *Teaching: A Course in Applied Psychology.* Chicago: Science Research Associates, Inc., 1971. 466 pp. Bibliography.

This superior collection of readings is designed as a college text for courses in educational psychology, child development, and special education. The articles are well organized so that students are exposed to theoretical issues as well as to teaching techniques.

Order from: Science Research Associates, Inc.
259 East Erie Street
Chicago, Illinois 60611
($6.40 plus postage, paperback)

Becker, Wesley C., Engelmann, Siegfried, and Thomas, Don R., *Teaching: A course in Applied Psychology.* Chicago: Science Research Associates, Inc., 1971. 466 pp. Bibliography.

This book is for teachers and teachers-in-training. It presents teaching technology in a way that will enable a teacher to run an effective classroom. The first section of the book deals with the use of consequences in the class. The second section deals with concept formation, and presents a model of teacher-child interaction that will result in concept acquisition.

Don Dorsey is a former elementary teacher in the behavior analysis follow through project in Philadelphia, Pennsylvania. He is currently completing the Ph. D. in developmental psychology in the Department of Human Development, University of Kansas, Lawrence, Kansas.

Order from: Science Research Associates, Inc.
259 East Erie Street
Chicago, Illinois 60611
($6.95 plus postage)

Becker, Wesley C., Thomas, Don R., and Carnine, Douglas, *Reducing Behavior Problems: An Operant Conditioning Guide for Teachers*. Urbana, Ill.: ERIC Clearinghouse on Early Childhood Education, 1969. 37 pp. Bibliography.

Emphasis is on preschool and elementary children. This brief pamphlet provides a good introduction to the methods and results pioneering classroom behavior modification studies.

Order from: Educational Resources Information Center
National Laboratory on Early Childhood Education
805 West Pennsylvania Avenue
Urbana, Illinois 61801
($1.50 plus postage)

Benson, Arthur M., ed., *Modifying Deviant Social Behaviors in Various Classroom Settings*. Eugene, Ore.: Department of Special Education, College of Education, University of Oregon, 1969. 80 pp. Bibliography.

Detailed procedures for behavior modification in different classroom settings with charts and data of experimental results of pioneering classroom behavior modification studies. as Agents of Change in the Classroom," and "Special Class Placement as a Treatment Alternative for Deviant Behavior in Children."

Order from: Department of Special Education
College of Education
University of Oregon
Eugene, Oregon 97403
($2.15 including postage)

Berman, Mark L., ed., *Motivation and Learning: Applying Contingency Management Techniques*. Englewood Cliffs, N. J.: Educational Technology Publications, Inc., 1971. 195 pp. Bibliography.

A collection of papers covering many topics in behavior management. Most selections are written for people with some background in reinforcement theory, which makes this book difficult first reading. One of the most interesting features is a list of the names and addresses of people active in behavior modification work.

Order from: Educational Technology Publications, Inc.
Englewood Cliffs, New Jersey 07632
($3.95)

Blackham, G. and Silberman, A., *Modification of Child Behavior: Principles and Procedures*. Belmont, Calif.: Wadsworth Publishing Company, Inc., 1970. 186 pp. Bibliography.

Describes and analyzes more than 40 problems of major concern to teachers, counselors, and parents. Deals with elementary grade children.

Order from: Wadsworth Publishing Company, Inc.
              Belmont, California 94002
              ($4.50 including postage)

Blackwood, Ralph O., *Operant Control of Behavior: Elimination of Misbehavior and Motivation of Children*. Akron Ohio: Exordium Press, 1971. 240 pp. Bibliography.

A thorough yet clear explanation of how teachers can use behavioral techniques to improve their classes. The book covers almost all aspects of classroom management, and the author assures success if his methods are followed.

Order from: Exordium Press
              Box 606
              Akron, Ohio 44308
              ($4.47 plus postage)

Bradfield, Robert H., ed., *Behavior Modification: The Human Effort*. San Rafael, Calif.: Dimension Publishing Co., 1970. 218 pp.

A collection of essays with a major emphasis on behavior modification in educational settings. The book includes two sections concerning moral and philosophical aspects of changing behavior.

Order from: Dimensions Publishing Company
              Box 4221
              San Rafael, California 94903
              ($4.95)

Buckley, Nancy K. and Walker, Hill M., *Modifying Classroom Behavior: A Manual of Procedures for Classroom Teachers*. Champaign, Ill.: Research Press Company, 1970. 124 pp.

A small readable book for teachers and teachers-in-training that explains the principles of behavior in clear nontechnical terms. The book is semiprogrammed, and requires active responding throughout.

Order from: Research Press Company
              2612 North Mattis Avenue
              Champaign, Illinois 61820
              ($4.00, discounts on large orders)

Deibert, Alvin N. and Harmon, Alice J., *New Tools for Changing Behavior*. Champaign, Ill.: Research Press Company, 1970. 136 pp. Bibliography.

A breezy, well written book that states behavioral principles in a clear exciting way. There are questions to fill in on every page, as well as many interesting case histories.

Order from: Research Press Company
2612 North Mattis Avenue
Champaign, Illinois 61820
($4.00, discounts on large orders)

Fargo, George A., Behrns, Charlene, and Nolen, Patricia, *Behavior Modification in the Classroom*. Belmont, Calif.: Wadsworth Publishing Company, Inc., 344 pp. 1970.

Readings selected to demonstrate classroom-relevant principles of behavior modification. Deals with ethical considerations, applications to a broad range of academic and nonacademic problem behaviors, as well as the uses of behavioral techniques by professionals other than teachers.

Order from: Wadsworth Publishing Company, Inc.
Belmont, California 94002
($4.95 plus postage)

Hall, R. Vance, *Managing Behavior, Parts I, II, and III*. Lawrence, Kansas: H & H Enterprises, Inc., 1971.

Three short volumes for instructing parents and teachers on principles of modifying behavior. The first volume deals with measuring behavior, the second with behavior principles, and the third with practical applications at home and at school. These volumes are technical, and it is easier to begin with part III, then read part II, then part I.

Order from: H & H Enterprises, Inc.
P. O. Box 3342
Lawrence, Kansas 66044
($1.55 per part, plus postage)

Hamblin, Robert L., Buckholdt, David, Ferritor, Daniel, Kozloff, Martin, and Blackwell, Lois, *The Humanization Processes: A Social, Behavioral Analysis of Childrens' Problems*. New York: John Wiley & Sons, Inc., 1971. 286 pp. Bibliography.

Describes the application of behavioral techniques to a wide range of problems in inner-city classrooms, with autistic children, with a hyperaggressive child, and with normal children. There is a good deal of theory in the book, but the authors have written for the educated and interested layman.

The clear prose and interesting examples make this serious reading a pleasant task.

Order from: John Wiley & Sons, Inc.
605 Third Avenue
New York, N. Y. 10016
($12.50)

Harris, Mary B., ed., *Classroom Uses of Behavior Modification.* Columbus, Ohio: Charles E. Merrill Publishing Company, 1972. 433 pp.

An excellent collection of pertinent classroom studies that can be read by teachers, education students, psychology students, and used as a college text. The studies are preceded by sections on research problems and principles of behavior modification, which aim to give readers critical faculties for research evaluation. The wide range of ages and problems discussed in the collection makes it especially useful.

Order from: Charles E. Merrill Publishing Company
1300 Alum Creek Drive
Columbus, Ohio 43216
($5.95)

Homme, Lloyd, Casanyi, Attila P., Gonzales, Mary Ann, and Rechs, James R., *How to Use Contingency Contracting in the Classroom* (rev. ed.). Champaign, Ill.: Research Press Company, 1971. 130 pp.

A how-to manual for teachers. Using a programmed format, it shows in stepwise fashion how the contract can be used effectively to apply a basic behavioral principle.

Order from: Research Press Company
2612 North Mattis Avenue
Champaign, Illinois 61820
($3.75)

Klein, Roger D., Kapkiewicz, Walter G., and Roden, Aubrey H., eds., *Behavior Modification In Educational Settings.* Springfield, Ill.: Charles C Thomas, Publisher, 1973. 551 pp.

This large collection of readings is aimed at giving teachers the skills to cope with academic or behavior problems that arise in most classrooms. Since a wide variety of problems, and many types of students are featured, teachers should find this a useful reference. Because the articles come from journals and papers read at conferences, the book is demanding reading.

Order from: Charles C Thomas, Publisher
Bannerstone House
301-327 East Lawrence Avenue
Springfield, Illinois 62717
($14.95)

Madsen, Charles H., Jr., and Madsen, Clifford K., *Teaching/ Discipline: Behavioral Principles Toward a Positive Approach.* Boston: Allyn & Bacon, Inc., 1970. 136 pp. Bibliography

Shows teachers how to gain control of their classrooms without resorting to coercion. It is meant for everyday use, and it contains clear instructions for teachers. The suggestions in this book are quite practical, and there are no pie-in-the-sky approaches to discipline.

Order from: Allyn & Bacon, Inc.
College Order Department
Rockleigh, New Jersey 07647
($3.95, discounts on large orders)

Madsen, Clifford K., and Madsen, Charles H. Jr., *Parents/ Children/Discipline: A Positive Approach.* Boston: Allyn & Bacon, Inc., 1972. 213 pp.

The authors show how parents can be loving and yet discipline their children. The secret is to catch the children being good rather than being bad. Parents can change children's behavior first by observing the act, then placing a consequence on the act, and finally by evaluating the effect of the consequences. The Madsens are not pro child, but pro family; and they are softies enough to entitle the final chapter "Loving — The Art of Discipline."

Order from: Allyn & Bacon, Inc.
College Order Department
Rockleigh, New Jersey 07647
($3.95)

Meacham, Merle L., and Wiesen, Allen E., *Changing Classroom Behavior, A Manual for Precision Teaching.* Scranton, Pa.: International Textbook Company, 1969. 212 pp. Bibliography.

A readable and practical guide to precision teaching with many examples of applications in the normal classroom as well as chapters on working with the retarded, the socially deprived, and the emotionally disturbed child. Emphasis on "humanistic behaviorism and ethics."

Order from: International Textbook Company
Scranton, Pennsylvania 18515
($2.95)

O'Leary, K. Daniel, and O'Leary, Susan G., eds., *Classroom Management: The Successful Use of Behavior Modification.* New York: Pergamon Press Inc., 1972. 659 pp. Bibliography.

The O'Learys have assembled a very useful book for anyone in education: teachers, school psychologists, administrators, or education students. An overview of applied psychology in education is followed by 37 articles printed in full. The reading is difficult, but worthwhile.

Order from: Pergamon Press Inc.
Maxwell House, Fairview Park
Elmsford, New York 10523
($5.95 paperback, $12.50 hardcover)

Patterson, Gerald R., and Gullion, M. Elizabeth, *Living with Children: New Methods for Parents and Teachers.* Champaign, Ill.: Research Press Company, 1968. 117 pp.

A programmed book especially designed for parents to help them learn to deal with their children's behavior problems with simple techniques. Authors worked with many families while preparing the book, which includes sample behavior charts.

Order from: Research Press Company
2612 North Mattis Avenue
Champaign, Illinois 61820
($3.00 plus postage)

Pitts, Carl E., *Introduction to Educational Psychology.* New York: Thomas Y. Crowell Company, Inc., 1971. 231 pp.

A college level text that draws heavily on the principles of behavior and reinforcement theory in the context of examining the scientific process at work in the educational setting. Combines reprinted readings with discussions of both cognitive and affective learning objectives and techniques of evaluation.

Order from: Thomas Y. Crowell Company, Inc.
201 Park Avenue South
New York, N. Y. 10003
($5.95)

Semb, George, with Green, Donald R., Hawkins, Robert P., Michael, Jack, Phillips, Elery L., Sherman, James A., Sloane, Howard, and Thomas, Don R., eds., *Behavior Analysis and Education — 1972.* Lawrence, Kan.: Department of Human Development, 1972. 415 pp.

This book is a collection of papers from the Third Annual Conference on Behavior Analysis in Education. The papers present studies from pre-school through the university level, including Special Education. The behaviors modified range through arithmetic achievement, composition writing, spelling, and creative painting. This collection includes sections on teacher training, and the use of students to modify the behavior of other students. The inclusion of a paper on physician administered drugs in the classroom, and one on values in behavior modification make this collection diverse, current, and comprehensive.

Order from: Department of Human Development
University of Kansas
Lawrence, Kansas 66044
($4.98)

Sheppard, William C., Shank, Steven B., and Wilson, Darla, *How to be a Good Teacher: Training Social Behavior in Young Children*. Champaign, Ill.: Research Press Company, 1972. 91 pp.

This is a nice guide book for teachers of young children. The text uses many changes in typography to direct attention to important ideas. The unusual format makes this book easy on the eyes.

Order from: Research Press Company
2612 North Mattis Avenue
Champaign, Illinois 61820
($3.00, discounts on large orders)

Skinner, B. F., *The Technology of Teaching*. New York: Appleton-Century-Crofts, 1968. 264 pp.

A well written, stimulating book by the discoverer of the principle out of which behavior modification techniques have grown. Not concerned especially with classroom behavior, it is rather, an attempt to rethink the whole educational enterprise in terms of reinforcement. Chapter titles include: "The Science of Learning and the Art of Teaching," "Why Teachers Fail," and "Discipline, Ethical Behavior, and Self-Control."

Order from: Appleton-Century-Crofts
440 Park Avenue South
New York, N. Y. 10016
($3.25 paperback, $6.00 hardback)

Sulzer, Beth, and Mayer, G. Roy, *Behavior Modification Procedures for School Personnel*. Hinsdale, Ill.: The Dryden Press, Inc., 1972. 320 pp.

A college text that aims to help teachers motivate students, and provide teachers with management and instructional techniques. This concise and clearly written book is full of specific suggestions for introducing and evaluating new classroom procedures.

Order from: Dryden Press, Inc.
901 North Elm
Hinsdale, Illinois 60521
($4.95)

Tharp, Roland G., and Wetzel, Ralph J., *Behavior Modification in the Natural Environment*. New York: Academic Press, Inc., 1969. 229 pp.

A thorough presentation of behavior modification principles as applied to behaviorally disordered children. Offers many practical suggestions, numerous examples.

Order from: Academic Press, Inc.
111 Fifth Avenue
New York, N. Y. 10003
($10.00)

Webster, S. W., *Discipline in the Classroom*. San Francisco: Chandler Publishing Company, 1968. 142 pp. Bibliography.

The author includes behavior modification as only one of many techniques useful to the classroom teacher. After discussing the nature of discipline, the classroom environment, and the teacher's role, the author presents student behavior problems, five of them elementary and five of them secondary students, with evaluations of each situation by two or three experienced teachers, and invites the reader to draw his own conclusions.

Order from: Science Research Associates, Inc.
259 East Erie Street
Chicago, Illinois 60611
($2.70)

Whaley, Donald L. and Malott, Richard W., *Elementary Principles of Behavior*. New York: Appleton-Century-Crofts, 1971. 446 pp.

An excellent book that covers basic behavioral principles in clearly written language. Whaley and Malott are the Rowan and Martin of psychology, so tears of laughter may obscure your vision when reading this very lively introduction to behavioral psychology.

Order from: Appleton-Century-Crofts
440 Park Avenue South
New York, N. Y. 10016
($7.45)

Index